Fringe Locations
True & Fictional Stories

Also by Eric G. Müller

Novels:
Rites of Rock
Meet Me at the Met
The Black Madonna and the Young Sculptor: Mythic Dimensions of Celtic Chartres

Children's Books:
The Invisible Boat (Volume I)
The Invisible Boat and the Molten Dragon (Volume II)
Tiny Tin Elf ~ (illustrated by Ella Manor Lapointe)

Nonfiction:
Drops on the Water: Stories of Growing Up from a Father and Son (Coauthor: Matthew Zanoni Müller)
Do You Love Your Teachers? Memoir of a Waldorf Teacher
The Waldorf Main Lesson

Poetry
Coffee on the Piano for You
Frogs, Frags, & Kisses
Life Poems for my Students
Pilgrim Poet ~ Roaming Rebel
Truth, Lies, & Light (published under Elryn Westerfield)

Play
Rounding the Cape of Good Hope

Fringe Locations

True & Fictional Stories

By
Eric G. Müller

*To all those wonderful people who have
touched and enriched my life in one way or another*

All rights reserved. No part of this book may be reproduced or transmitted in any manner, without prior permission by the publisher, except for purposes of research, review, criticism, or private study. Some names, places, and sequences have been changed in the non-fiction stories

Printed with the support of the Alkion Press Fund

ISBN: 978-1-7340170-7-6

Copyright © 2021 Eric G. Müller

First Edition
Printed in the USA

Published in 2021 by Alkion Press
14 Old Wagon Road, Ghent, NY 12075
www.alkion-press.com

Title: Fringe Locations: True & Fictional Stories
Author: Eric G. Müller
www.ericgmuller.com
Cover photos: Martina Angela Müller

Contents

PART ONE
Fiction

The Red Wind ~ 1
Hotel Pischa ~ 12
Sundial ~ 13
Pool Cleaner in the Yucatan ~ 16
Up in Smoke ~ 24
Optimistic Freshman ~ 28
Yeah, I Killed my Girlfriend ~ 30
4' 33" ~ 33
Fringe Location ~ 35

PART TWO
Non-Fiction

Draft Dodger ~ 51
A Walk through Time and Snow ~ 57
Allen Ginsberg at the Atlantis ~ 60
Stromboli ~ 68
7 Trains, 7 Planes: *A Blessing* ~ 75
"Water, Water" ~ 83
We Met at The Met ~ 85
Thumbing Down the Road ~ 95

Glossary ~ 129
Acknowledgements ~ 131
Publication Credits ~ 131
About the Author ~ 132

PART ONE

FICTION

The Red Wind

JAGERSFONTEIN: A bony and sun-beaten *dorp,* ruffled within the sprawling *veld* and reachless sky. Midafternoon: the corrugated roofed houses, wide dusty streets and starched churches, remain mute, inert – apart from the anomalous sounds of a single piano issuing from a small brick house. On the outskirts: mine dumps – grey tombstones of the world's oldest diamond mine, reminders of better days, when "jagger" diamonds had turned the outpost into a boomtown, yielding the world's clearest and biggest exemplars: The 'Excelsior Stone,' the 'Reitz diamond,' amongst others. The diamond rush around the prosperous 'Big Hole' was short lived, and decades later Jagersfontein was once again reduced to a forgotten district in South Africa's interior, unheeded – a *Boere stad.*

Mid 1940s, just before Germany's capitulation: three of them in the living room, sparsely furnished but cozy. Faint fragrance of newly watered geraniums from the mantlepiece merge with the lingering odor of the midday meal: toad in the hole and sauerkraut.

Seated, the father, fragile, in an armchair, close to the cold empty fireplace. Legs crossed, the floppy khaki trousers tucked tight around his thin thighs and knobby knees; sockless feet pushed into well-worn leather slippers. His white shirt is spotless, frayed at the collar, buttoned up to the sagging neck, his orange paisley necktie hanging off duty and loose. Plain golden cufflinks adorn the shirt sleeves, accentuating the blue-veined arabesque of his hands. Face, translucent, mapped with myriad fine lines, the sensitive contours enhanced by slim, silver framed spectacles and a smoky halo of silky thinning hair, parted unevenly through the middle, puffy wisps extending over his ears. Eyes, a brittle blue. Only the eyebrows hint at determination, arched sternly above the level nose, dented above the bridge. A few deep-cut wrinkles fork into his pale purple lips, which hint at tears never wept. The rilled hands are sunk comfortably in his lap within each other's loyal hold. His head, held high, reminiscent of a bird's, is lost in memories – the aging father, German, into the fifth year of his 'soft internment.'

The mother, ensconced on the couch, sewing. On her right, an open-lidded rattan basket muddled with buttons, colored cotton reels, rubber bands, needles, well-stocked pink pin cushion, name tags, zippers, and more. On her left, a pile of clothes waiting to be mended, darned, made whole. Her legs, thick calved, hover slightly above the wood floor, the wool slippered feet quivering faintly to the rhythm of her pulse. Her brown and airy calico dress with a wide creamy collar, edged with crocheted lace, ripples and whispers at the slightest movement. A jade brooch glistens above her left breast. The waves of grey hair are held in place by two mother of pearl combs and an almost imperceptible hairnet. She is knitting socks, her breath aligned to the regular clicks of the needles, the mouth apart, her tongue resting along the lower row of her false teeth. The green eyes are always ready to laugh and respond kindly to the world – the mother who used to live in the bustling city of Durban.

By the piano, a girl of thirteen, the daughter – a *laatlammetjie*. Tiny feet in white socks and shiny black sandals that intermittently tip down on the pedals like a ballerina. The arms move with ease over the ivory keys, the fingers fluid, setting tones adrift with a musical intelligence beyond her tender age. A few years back she'd won competitions, performed concertos in Durban; a child prodigy. Piles of music lie on and next to the Grotrian-Steinweg upright. But now she plays by heart, the music streaming through her slender body from the periphery, down and along the ivory keys, the wood and felt hammers, the taut metal strings, until the sounds drain into the large iron frame, the melodies whirling around the sound box, before lifting off – unlocked and freed from bondage. They fill, then spread outward through the brick walls, toward arcane peripheries – alive, active, imperceptibly changing the *dorp* and veld outside. She's going through her favorite pieces, mostly sonatas by angelic Mozart, 'Papa' Haydn, and swarthy Beethoven, with a smattering of Bach preludes or a Schubert impromptu. Her earnest face intermittently melts into smiles that reflect the nuance of mood inherent in the respective motifs. A red silk ribbon holds her undulating and thick mahogany hair together in a long and lax pony tail. On either side, her parents, not so much hearing the music as absorbing it, note for silvery note. The daughter, who could have been their granddaughter.

"Christa?" It is the mother, now with threaded needle, bending over a blouse. There is no immediate response, and none expected. Christa always plays a piece through to the end, rarely letting herself be rushed. Ending the Beethoven bagatelle, the petite girl relaxes her upright posture and stares dreamily up at the bust of Chopin on top of the black lacquered piano next to the brown pyramidal wooden metronome, before spinning around on her adjustable piano stool.

"Yes, Mom?" Her clear face broadens into a smile, two dimples emerging. Another pause as the mother grunts the finishing touches to the newly sewn hem, before her hands flop over it in finality. "Done it." She looks over at Christa, who is swiveling gently back and forth on her stool. "Sorry to interrupt your playing, but would you go down to the grocery store and get a few things?"

"Now?" She twirls back to face the piano and starts playing 'In the Mood,' singing, "Sure, just tell me what you want, 'cause *I'm in the mood now.*" She ends the jaunty piece with a flourish, which makes her father smile, clap twice, before interlacing his fingers and returning to his reverie.

"Not much." She's smiling, eyes pressed together with crinkled mirth. "Just some *mielie-meal*, a loaf of bread, some washing powder… oh, and a quart of milk and a pound of sugar. But you will have to go now because 'Jasbecks' will be closing soon."

"I'll go now-now," and she plays 'The Sandwich' by Mozart, getting faster and faster until she jumps up with the swipe of the last chord, immediately hopping around to her father's side, giving him a kiss on the cheek, which is returned with a faint smile and a soft pat on her shoulder. "I'll need some money, Mom."

"My bag is in the kitchen. Hurry now, my *goggatjie*."

Christa skips into the kitchen, rummages for a few bills and coins in the ostrich leather handbag, grabs a basket from the pantry and runs out the backdoor shouting, "Bye," over her shoulder.

"I'll have tea ready when you get back," she hears her mother's muted voice as she rushes to the shed. Under the fragrant jacaranda tree, she stops to sniff the scented air, tentatively, then deeply, her skin prickling with appreciation. A gust of cool wind blows loose flowers down from the blooming tree, several landing on her head and shoulders. With the second gust she wonders whether to run back and fetch a jersey. The Karoo can get chilly in the evenings. Instead, she hurries on, wheeling her red bicycle from the dark shed.

It's a ten-minute ride along corrugated and potholed dirt roads, and it is with relief that she approaches Jasbecks, the Lebanese trading store. She freewheels to a halt, dismounts hastily, leans the bike against the front wall, and wriggles the basket from the handlebars. As an afterthought she brushes some of the red dust from her black sandals and white socks as best she can. About to enter, her attention is caught by the whimper of a tattered ridgeback who is tethered to a *witgat* tree with a short leather thong.

Hesitatingly, she watches the dog's desperate struggle, gnawing at the reem, froth forming around his mouth. Noticing her, he stops his freedom fight and stares intently at her with his clear agate eyes, one leg lifted questioningly, the slender tail venturing a wag in the hope of release. She knows that ridgebacks love to hunt and run – to be free. Feeling helpless she enters the shop, muttering, "Poor thing."

Christa steps from of the stark afternoon glare into the dark, cool and dense interior. As always, she flinches at the ill composed smells – the acrid odors of cleaning detergents, musty blankets, moldy perishables, stale tobacco, dusty tools, cookers, paraffin lamps. Wrinkling her nose, she hesitates and glances over at Jasbeck's son, who's about her age, seated behind the counter. He's sunk into a Superman comic, loudly masticating a fistful of *Chappies* chewing

The Red Wind

gum, blowing and popping bubbles. A chrome transistor radio, wheezy with static, pops songs on the metal shelf above him, next to silver-wrapped rolls of chewing tobacco and yellow bulk-packs of Lion Matches. His slick black hair is held in place by a generous dab of Brylcreem, in perfect imitation of the superhero. He does not look up from the garish thrill pages, as her meek entrance darkens the doorway, casting a plaintive shadow over him. She stands a little at a loss, feeling like she's intruding. Quietly she treads to the rear of the shop, away from being ignored. Her eyes quickly accustom themselves to the dark, and she moves down the narrow aisles, the shelves crammed with an abundance of cheapness – a trinket museum of antiquated necessities and kitsch luxuries. Rows of *biltong* and reels soft sticky black-studded flycatchers hang between carcasses of cheap steel string guitars: the muddy brown ones and the smoky condensed milk white guitars with grey clouds flitting across. She inevitably bumps into them, releasing hollow moans. Looking at the plastic blowup beachballs and colorful buckets and spades, she wonders who would buy them, so far removed from any ocean or beach.

Hastily she grabs what she needs, adds a packet of gingerbread biscuits to sweeten teatime, and plonks the groceries on the counter in front of the lip-smacking Superboy, his chewing chin still juddering like an automaton. He does not look up. He never does and she wishes jovial Mr. Jasbeck was serving her. Jasbeck senior always tells jokes and makes customers feel welcome. She stares impatiently at the boy, annoyed. The comic's cover catches her interest for a fleeting moment: Superman flying over a burning city and getting zapped by bolts of lightning. *How stupid*, she thinks, fascinated nonetheless, never having read a comic before. With the turning of the page the boy deigns to become aware of her and squints up, his eyes filmed over, in another world. Going through the items he presses the prices into the till with his lubberly fingers until the cash register's bell clangs in finality. She hands him the money. He feeds the register, rams it shut, and flies back to super-world. She quickly packs the items into the basket and hurries out, back into rigid

Part One

brightness. Remembering the ridgeback, she turns toward him, but the dog's gone, the cord chewed right through. Though glad for the dog, she's disappointed, having wanted to cuddle him, maybe even exchange a few comforting words. Christa wiggles the filled basket onto the handlebars, turns the bike around and starts to peddle homewards. She chooses a shortcut along the outskirts of town, past the mine dumps, though the difference is negligible: at most a minute. But it makes for a change.

She's alone on the road. No cars, farmer's bakkie, or Africans to wave to. Eyes on the gravel, she watches out for orange clods and the unavoidable corrugated strips, formed by the back-and-forth of cloudbursts and dry heat. The chain rattles wildly against the mudguard, and her whole body is jolted through. She fares no better in the sandy areas, the wheels losing traction, slowing her down. A smooth stretch promises temporary relief, giving her a chance to lift her head and relax. Seconds later she barely misses two fast slithering snakes that cross her path. She slows down, passing a row of shacks to her left that had once sheltered workers, but now stand empty, dilapidated. To her right, a smaller mine dump, appearing like a molehill in the vast expanse of veld; a dehumanized deserted tract, a scab in the arid wasteland, waiting in vain to be plowed, irrigated, and tended. From the town's center she hears the church bell crack five times, the brittle tintinnabulations getting stuck like splinters in the scrubby veld. She pushes for more speed. A sudden crust of wind peels off sharply, snatching the back wheel. The bike lurches dangerously. She squeals, wrestling with the handlebars in a fierce attempt to keep her balance, legs outstretched for support. She regains control, the basket thumping against the front mudguard. She pushes down hard on the pedals. The wind squall gives up and dissolves. Not a grass helm stirs.

Her lengthening shadow looms out in front of her as the sun treks resolutely towards the horizon behind her. This dark partner offers little consolation, who, with perfect agility adapts to the slightest change, mocking her movements like a distorted puppet. Yet, she fancies seeing colors circulating through its darkling presence, caused by the dance of weariness from the sneak attack. Out of the corner of her eye she spots two grey goshawks flying fast in the opposite direction, vanishing in the screen of setting light. The ride has never taken so long.

As she pedals along, she thinks of Mozart whose melodies are never far from her mind. She pictures the maestro walking through a verdant cherry orchard, popping those sweet deep-red marbles into his mouth, delicately held between the thumb and forefinger, composing melodies triggered by the intensities of taste. Out of a curious impulse, she shouts, "Amadeus, throw your wig to the wind, rip off your fancy jacket, tear your frilly shirt from your torso, kick your bronze buckled boots across the manicured lawn. Snatch instead a *knobkerrie* and saunter, bare chested, across the African veld. Hey *Wolferl*, how would that make you feel?" She laughs, picturing the scene, though the unchecked utterance takes her by surprise. To avoid further fanciful ramblings, she lifts herself off the saddle, leans forward with the full weight of her lithe body, and pushes down hard on the pedals. Her intention, however, is checked almost instantaneously by a cluster of potholes, forcing her to maneuver the bike in haphazard zigzags, chain rattling like a hacking cough, hair coming undone, the red ribbon fluttering off into the dust behind her. She can scarcely keep steady, which infuriates her. Then, instead of dodging the holes, she steers straight ahead along the deeply rutted road, yelling with fierce determination, "Master Mozart, what symphonies would you have composed… what diabolical concertos, had you lived here, having only known deserts and *dongas*, open veld or dense and tangled jungles? What orchestras would then have dared to perform your works?" Her words shudder and shiver through her rattled frame. "What genius would have possessed you? How would the world have coped with your creations?"

A startled meerkat jumps out in front of the slight girl with the fluttering hair. She pulls both handbrakes as tightly as she can: skids, misses, crashes – the groceries whirling and spilling through the air into the sand-scuffed soil. Dazed and sprawled over the ground she sees the hapless animal scuttle off to safety in the opposite direction, chased by a flash of wind. She gets up, rubs and slaps the dust from her blouse and dress. Blood trickles from her right knee and left elbow. Raising her fist into the air she shouts, "You'd hate it, Mozart, you'd hate it, hate it – this desolation, this emptiness, this wasteland." She gulps and wipes away slithering tears, leaving ochre streaks across the cheeks.

She scans the skies. In the distance, the horizon is bruised with clouds, but something about that inflating mass puzzles her. The rusty brown cumulus is unlike any she's seen before, swelling before her eyes. She bites her lips, rolls her tongue. Tiny dust devils appear from nowhere and cavort around her, before flitting away like crazy will o' the wisps across the *vlakte*. Suddenly she knows and names the nemesis: "Sandstorm!"

Of course: She recalls the writhing ridgeback chewing through the leather reem, the slithering snakes, the two raptors, the startled meerkat. They'd sensed the impending dust storm all along. The sudden realization sharpens all her senses. Nature, which had appeared so empty, dead and desolate just moments ago, erupts and heaves to life: Flocks of birds fly overhead; duikers dart nervously between acacias. Close by, *dassies* run for cover in rocky outcrops, midst a host of scurrying lizards, snakes, and waddling tortoises. Large herds of springbok emerge from the distance, hurtling, jumping and pronking through the air, leaving clouds of dust in their wake, accompanied by other antelopes. To her left, a galloping gemsbok thunders past. The *veld* has awakened: desperate fugitives seeking safety. *How could such barren terrain contain so much life? From where do they come?* Even the plants appear to be tugging at the ground to uproot themselves, pleading with the wind to whisk them away before the full force of the sandstorm is bound to devour them. As she peers around, transfixed and amazed, she mutters, "No, Amadé, I was wrong! You would have loved this."

No sooner said than a massive swarm of bees heads straight toward her, extending beyond the width of the road and reaching past the tops of telephone poles. Released from a momentary paralysis, she rips the basket from the crippled handlebars and sticks it hastily over her head. Just in time! The bees pelt and pop against the basket, her chest and shoulders. She drops down and hunches up on the dirt road, engulfed by the centripetal drone, the blood from her scraped knee oozing and dropping into the dusty earth, immediately absorbed like ink on blotting paper. *May the Queen Bee not land on me,* she thinks in quiet desperation. She'd be smothered by the whole hive if that were to happen. The pelting against the basket and body increases. She contracts herself into a tight taut ball like an armadillo. *Why didn't I see it coming – I should have sensed it like the animals.*

As quickly as it came, the buzzing barrage fades away, leaving her cocooned on the road – alone, unscathed. She peers cautiously out from under her basket-helmet, watching the swarm's embodied mind ascend toward the sinking sun like a lost soul seeking its source. Seconds later she jumps to her feet. In the dim rust-red east, the burgeoning sandstorm now rages hundreds of feet into the sky. The colossal wave covers the entire horizon, rolling towards her – a tsunami of wind-tossed sand. Sundry lightning flashes zip through the murky lower regions. Unbridled squalls snarl and tug at her. She drops the basket and runs, leaving the spilled groceries and her mangled red bicycle beside the road, looking like a monster mantis. Tiny twisters lash out and give chase. In her wake she hears the plangent roar of the encroaching beast – smells the static.

Tears drip from her face as she sprints homeward, leaving minute craters in the dust behind her. And as she runs with the densifying wind and sand closing in, the nebulous disorder of her soul swells and clears. The sound of the storm merges with the soft thuds of her sandaled feet as they flit over the gravel. Nature's macro-rhythm unites with the pace of her lean limbs, rapid panting, and surging blood that pulses through her heaving head and chest. Like a blossoming flower she senses herself opening up, welcoming the unfolding lucidity, while succumbing to a higher power with devotional abandon. She ignores the storm's temporal fermentations, the stinging red heads of sand biting into her, the tentacled wind sucking and curling round her heels. She feels nothing but sounds unleashed, and experiences the voice of the storm as a mighty choir streaming through her, each grain of sand a peal of victory; she hears a battle conducted with smiting gongs of determination, a majestic rage, harmonized to ignite the terrestrial elements into sweeping motions – the words of the invisibles elevated into song, Gaia's impulsive choral performed in lawful consequence to the human mind withered with doubt and prejudice, necessitating the maelstrom. Instead of submission she hears tonal triumph. *Beethoven would have loved this too*, she thinks as she runs, stumbles, falls.

The three of them in the living room. It is late. The storm has passed. A pot of tea, wedges of diagonally cut sandwiches, and a bowl of buttermilk rusks are neatly arranged on a tray by the curtained window, untouched. A small fire crackles in the hearth, flames pursuing wisps of smoke up the chimney. A paraffin lamp gives off ambient light.

"Do you think she'll be alright?" It is the voice of the mother, sitting left of the couch on the piano stool.

"She'll be fine. It's best to let her rest." The father leans forward in his armchair.

"Shame, the poor goggatjie getting caught up in that horrible storm." She strokes her daughter's cheeks who's lying on the couch, eyes closed, still dressed in her dust-covered skirt and blouse; her elbow and knee wrapped in gauze, spots of red seeping through.

"We can be so thankful that the worst part of the sandstorm spared us, though it will take a while to clear all the debris... restore electricity."

"How lucky that you found her so quickly... that she was so close to home. Poor thing."

"More than luck, I believe." He sits back in his armchair. "Do you recall," – his voice fades into the distance – "that sandstorm we had before the war? Just like this it was." He scratches his chin. "Haven't had one like that since, have we?"

"No, we haven't." The mother feels her sleeping daughter's forehead. "Do you really think she is alright?"

"I remember how uneasy that storm had made me feel. Like nature's warning of doom to come. And it really did turn out to be an admonition of death, didn't it? A red and bloody wind before the war. And us, now… interned, forced to live here in this God forsaken place." He breathes deeply, ruffling his hand through his poufy white hair. "What does it portend? I fear no good will come of this storm."

"No Dad, no!" It's the voice of the daughter, eyes blinking, pushing herself up from the couch.

"Easy, easy, Christa, lie down again. You've had quite a shock. You could have died."

"But Dad, I must tell you, really," – her eyes are wide open and bright – "I heard it singing, I heard the storm's music… it was so… I don't know… liberating! Dad, Mom, if we could sing like that while it storms…" She falls back on the couch. "Really, it's going to be alright."

Hotel Pischa

WHEN I WAS FIVE years old, my father left us to live in the Swiss Alps. He booked into the luxurious Hotel Pischa that overlooked the quaint town of Davos – a coveted village for the rich and famous, renowned for its winter sports. Our house in Basel felt empty after he moved out, and my older brother and I found it unfair that he lived in the lap of luxury while my mother struggled to make ends meet. Every time she got off the phone with him, she cried. It took six months before he invited us to come up and see him. We were excited, glued to the window as we traveled by train, watching the dreary landscape give way to forests, lakes and snow-covered peaks.

He welcomed us outside the hotel with a big smile, handing my brother and me a Swiss pocket knife. He looked thinner than I had remembered him, but he had a tan. "I have my own balcony where I sit every day soaking up the sun," he said, laughing. But he didn't invite us in, though we begged. Instead, we went for a long walk along the promenade above the hotel. Soon he tired and we turned in at the nearest *Gaststube* and ordered *röschti* and *Apfelchorle*. My mother sat close to him and I hoped they might patch things up. Back on the train my brother blurted out, "I hate Dad for leaving us."

Mom put her hand on his arm. "He never wanted to leave us. Hotel Pischa is really a sanatorium. He's very ill – tuberculosis. This week he is going into surgery."

Sundial

HER RING FINGER MOVES back and forth along the lip of the Burgundy wine glass. Slowly. Her tongue touches her chapped upper lip, mirroring the movement. She sits in a leather wingback armchair, covered with three alpaca wool blankets that have lost their color. Her eyes peer through horn-rimmed glasses and are fixed on a crack in the velvet curtain. A slit of light steals through. Motes of dust swim in and out of the guillotine shaft that cuts across the solid mahogany table with upturned spindle legs. But no banquets have entertained any guests here for years. The stone fireplace, library and baby grand are in darkness.

Her hand slides down the stem of the glass. The thumb and middle finger caress the slim, transparent neck. Her puffed eyes are mesmerized by the specks of dust floating in the funnel of light. She wriggles her toes, covered by blue, frayed, woolen socks. They crack. Imperceptibly, the blade of light inches across the table. When it reaches the edge of the overhanging top, she swirls the wine and lifts the tapered glass to her parting mouth, sniffs the released aroma, and takes a sip. The tilted crystal bowl remains between her lips as she swallows. She swallows. Her tongue dips and tests the red puddle. She savors the tingle, and then sips again. Her left ear pops and she blinks. The third sip empties the glass. She lets the tapered glass linger against her chin, licking the thin, transparent lip, tasting its cool, smooth edge. Once the delicate flavor of the wine has faded, she puts down the glass on the pedestal side table. Her eyes follow the slow shift of light while she rubs her nose. Having silenced the itch, she lets her hand rest on the bottle, her thumb rubbing its neck, gently. Outside a police siren wails, followed by an ambulance.

Part One

When the pre-recorded bells of St. Mary's chime twelve, she lifts the bottle and pours another glass. Her shaky hand spills a few drops on the lace tablecloth. It absorbs the spreading red like blotting paper. She grunts. She wipes her hand against the Scottish plait flannel pajama top before placing the bottle next to a cluster of empty replicas that wait like expectant bowling pins. The hand of light strikes the clock on the mantelpiece: 10:59. She hasn't wound it up these last six years. The constant tick-tock had affected her like the drip-drip-drip of Chinese water torture. She prefers deep-sea silence. Leaning to her right she clasps an unopened bottle by the throat. She mutters as she lifts it to her lap and screws into the cork with the opener. After opening the bottle, she places it on the pedestal, breathes deeply and sighs.

Her middle finger moves back and forth along the rim of the wine glass. Slowly. Her tongue touches her chapped upper lip, mirroring the movement. The edge of light now slices across the black and white photo of her husband, framed and hanging left of the clock. It was taken twenty years ago. His arm hangs around her shoulder, but she's still hidden in shadow. She lifts the glass to her lips and drinks, sip for sip to the last drop. Putting the glass back on the stained tablecloth she looks away as the beam of light now exposes her younger self in the photo – smiling, smoking and wearing a bikini. Again, she stares straight ahead at the wound in the curtains.

She pours herself another glass. The ray of light has moved on and is now playing on the ivory keys of the baby grand. She used to play and perform all around the world from the time she was nine. As a child prodigy they called her *Little Miss Lightning*, on account of her speed and virtuosity, both on and off the stage. The name stuck. She could elude the most rapacious paparazzi, and give instant and witty answers to any journalists or reporters. As a young woman she was the center of attention at any party, flirting and flitting from one man to the next, until she met her husband. The keys of the baby grand haven't been touched in seven years.

She empties one more glass and dozes off. Just after the fake bells toll two, the gash of light shines against the burgundy damask wallpaper, left of the fireplace. She does not want to look at the 5' by 8' rectangle that is darker than the rest of the wall. With trembling hand, she tops the glass with more wine. Again, she spills some drops over her fingers and onto the damp, embroidered tablecloth. Growling, she wipes her hand on the pajamas and impatiently downs the entire glass in seconds – a garish caricature of Little Miss Lightning. Yet, she cannot avert her eyes from the rectangle on the wall. Tears skew her sight. She removes the horn-rimmed glasses and wipes her eyes. A framed photo of her daughter hung in that spot until her husband removed it when he finally left – three years ago. Their daughter had died from massive internal injuries after falling out of the open window of their penthouse apartment. He forgot to shut it one morning after a brief airing – the very window behind the velvet curtain. It has never been opened since. But a slither of light always gets through, no matter how tightly she draws the curtain every morning. She had been off on tour at the time. She recalls opening the telegram in the lobby of a hotel in Tokyo. Or was it London? It's been eight years.

Her hand slips under the alpaca blanket and down the sides of the upholstered chair. She feels the pistol's cold barrel with her left hand; the pointer finger touches the front sight, and then enters the muzzle, simultaneously rubbing it up and down. Slowly she surrounds the cylinder with her thumb and forefinger, while her pinky curls around the trigger guard. She's panting. On most days she would push it back into the folds of the upholstery. Not today. Gripping the handle of the revolver she pulls it out from under the faded blanket. She's breathing heavily as she cocks the hammer and watches the cylinder revolve. The light from the curtain is no longer sharply defined. With her right hand she lifts the almost full bottle to her mouth and drinks as if she were drinking soda on a hot day, while the revolver rests in her lap, held by the left. Half emptied, she lets it sink while leisurely raising the handgun to her mouth. Her lips part and she pushes her tongue into the muzzle. The taste of metal merges with the tang of wine. Her finger tightens around the trigger. She lusts for light. She aches for air. Curtains could be parted, windows opened. She feels the muscles in her legs tightening. Mourning doves coo outside.

Pool Cleaner in the Yucatan

STACIE LOOKED OUT the airplane window. Last time she was in Cancun she got knocked up. That was fifteen years ago. An abortion, a string of boyfriends and a failed marriage lay between. Now she was a successful lawyer.

She stuck a stick of Wrigley's Spearmint into her mouth as they started to descend, hoping to avoid the inevitable pain in her ears during cabin pressure drop. She rummaged for her iPhone in her purse, plugged herself in, put it on shuffle and listened to snippets of songs, clicking to the next every few seconds. It was almost noon. She leaned back, closed her eyes, yawned, chewed vehemently and repeatedly swallowed saliva to counteract the pain. It helped to shorten the excruciating moments. You'd think by now aviation technology would have come up with something. She hated landings, and couldn't wait to be out of the plane, packed as it was with sassy students on spring break, raring to party. She'd booked her hotel months in advance to ensure a quiet room in the Golden Zone, just ten minutes from Cancun International airport by taxi.

The luxury resort was a massive futuristic looking ziggurat, and as soon as she entered her room she collapsed on the king-sized bed, panting through her mouth. She'd been up since 2 a.m. and apart from her clogged ears she had a splitting headache. She downed a second Tylenol, waited for relief to set in, and when it did, fell asleep.

The digital clock on her nightstand blinked 15:37 when she awoke. Stacie took a quick shower, slipped into an airy silk dress and went down to the bar for a quick espresso to clear her head and a piña colada to relax. The bar overlooked the serpentine pool that curved around two sides of the hotel – a resort out of reach for most students.

The summer before college she'd stayed in a budget hotel right in the center of Cancun – a week of beach, shopping, and night clubs, where she danced and drank till dawn. She'd been a straight A student throughout high school, rarely went out, and avoided parties. Her friends called her a party pooper and after graduation persuaded her to come along and "get a nightlife." Reluctantly she agreed. After she won the bikini contest, she was the star in her hotel. She hooked up with different guys every night, dancing and making-out – no further. As soon as the fondling began, she'd beat a fast retreat to the bathroom. Finally, she succumbed to the persistent onslaught of drink, charm and good looks of an exchange student from Oxford with a beguiling English accent. She let him into her heart and hotel room, where they stayed for the next three days.

Stacie ordered another piña colada. To think she'd caved in to a player – to someone who was nothing more than a cunning high school dropout from Atlantic City, New Jersey, who'd acquired his disarming *savior de vivre* by working the floor in various Casinos. She was angry all over again. On the last day they exchanged numbers and addresses with the promise to meet up. She had found her love. They called each other daily, but after she told him she was pregnant he ignored her calls and changed his cell phone number. E-mails and letters went unanswered. She went to Planned Parenthood, made an appointment and had the abortion.

Stacie found a lawn chair by the pool under a palm tree and smoked a cigarette. Her fingers trembled; her foot tapped the ground. For years she'd wanted to return to Cancun and visit the historic sites and natural wonders of the Yucatan Peninsula, but had always put it off, scared it would break open old wounds. Now, after all these years, she thought she'd left that all behind her – the pain and anger, those feelings of betrayal and the severe depression that had consumed her after the abortion, almost to the point of suicide. The relapse was like an erupting volcano, shooting suppressed memories out into the open. A few hours in Cancun, and already she regretted coming. *What was I thinking?*

Stacie got up and walked along the raked gravel path to the

Part One

gate leading to the beach. She flipped off her sandals. The white sand was hot and she jogged to the water's edge, letting the cool waves of low tide wash over her feet.

A week after the abortion she'd entered law school at Duke University and studied with a vengeance, graduating summa cum laude. She passed the bar exam with equal distinction.

She lit another cigarette, but almost immediately flicked it into the ocean and returned to her room. For five minutes she randomly flipped through TV channels, before hissing "Screw this." She flung the remote on the bed, put on her new sneakers and hopped on the first available shuttle bus to Cancun center.

Men had vied for her, and she enjoyed going out with any number of them, but at the slightest hint of anyone wanting her to commit, she broke it off. She was even more ruthless with herself, cutting off all contact the moment she developed feelings for someone. Nor did she stay long at any law firm. She'd started with a six-figure salary, and every change was a career move that came with a pay increase. She was willing to put in the time and work hard, confirmed by her résumé and glowing recommendations.

She'd met her husband in a criminal law firm in Albany, NY. He was a senior partner and she worked many cases with him. He was the only person whose work ethics matched hers. The two were relentless. Whatever case they worked on together they won. They could read each other's minds. A nod or a gesture between them was often all it took. No need for long discussions. Those who witnessed the proceedings in court or in meetings were unnerved. It was an almost mystical work relationship, which the couple mistook for love. They married with little fanfare, going to the marriage licensing bureau one Friday morning, only to return to work after a quick lunch at a fine restaurant. Two years later, when she accepted a job offer in one of the best law firms in Manhattan – too lucrative to refuse – the relationship fell apart. For six months she'd dutifully driven up to Albany on the weekends to be with him, but their marriage had no future. It was an amicable divorce.

Pool Cleaner in the Yucatan

Apart from new high-rise hotels and swanky shops, nothing much had changed in Cancun. Legions of students were already starting their club to club transmigrations. The industrial throb of loud music blared from all corners, merging with honking cars, shouts and laughter. She found refuge in the hush of an upscale restaurant and ordered coconut shrimp deep fried and a sparkling wine to go with the dish. She hoped a good dinner would restore her wits. Though excellent, she left most of the shrimp uneaten and returned to the hotel. She swallowed a sleeping pill and went to bed.

Over the last two years she hadn't traveled at all. She knew she needed a break. The prolonged bouts of insomnia had made her short tempered and impatient, especially towards her co-workers, but also to her clients. She forgot appointments and began to have little mishaps, such as locking herself out of her car or dropping her new iPhone from the balcony of her 16th floor apartment. It was clear: she had to get away – someplace where she could relax and do some sightseeing. The barista who prepared her mid-morning cappuccino had suggested the Yucatan Peninsula, raving about the ruins, cenotes, and great snorkeling. A fender-bender on the Saw Mill Parkway pushed her to buy the ticket.

The hotel offered daily excursions to the most popular tourist destinations, and the next day she did the Mayan Riviera tour. Though the stops at the underground caves of Rio Secreto, the ecological theme park at Xel-Ha, and the Mayan ruins at Tulum were spectacular, she found no joy. Her fraught nervous system resented the crowds, the tight schedule, and the shtick of the tour guides. She kept to herself and lingered behind the group, smoking when she could. On her return she cancelled the tour to Cozumel, an exotic island in the Caribbean. Instead, she rented a car for the week.

Knowing it was an almost hundred-mile trip to Chichén Itzá she left early in the morning, taking the main highway to Merida. At around 10:30, feeling the need for coffee and a bite to eat she turned off the highway onto the parallel running 'libre' road, which was more scenic, and passed through many villages. To her dismay the villages were rundown and displayed squalor and abject poverty.

Part One

Many of the houses were windowless shacks of cinder blocks and scrap materials such as plywood boards, plastic sheets and corrugated iron. Muddy yards were full of junk. Half-naked children ran around, shouting, laughing. A world at odds with the luxury resorts of Cancun. Stacie was uncomfortably aware at the discrepancy between the haves and have-nots. Entering another village, she slowed down. A man in a hammock caught her eye and waved, smiling. She quickly looked away, embarrassed, and accelerated. There were no cafes that looked inviting.

It was another 45 minutes before she noticed Kukulkan Restaurant & Bungalows, about ten miles from Chichén Itzá. She slammed on the breaks and parked in the shade of a large Guadalupe palm. The Garden Restaurant was surrounded by an array of tropical plants and royal palms that stretched over thirty feet high. Stacie sat down at one of the wooden tables under a palapa. Except for a family of four and an elderly couple who were enjoying a late breakfast the place was empty of customers. There wasn't a waiter in sight. Not three minutes had elapsed and already she felt annoyed at the lack of service, her leg shaking. As she lit a cigarette a shy teenage waitress came with the menu. Waving the menu aside Stacie ordered coffee and a Mexican omelet, "And add some avocados, please."

She glanced around. Above her some colorful birds were building nests in the thatch. A maid brought fresh linen to the cabañas at the far side of the expansive lawn. A plump iguana walked gawkily across the lawn toward the pool where a man collected leaves with a net attached to a long pole. Geckos chased each other up the wooden posts of the palapa. She leaned back and puffed on her cigarette, her eyes resting on the pool cleaner. Every movement was measured and in slow motion. She watched the net as it floated half over the water, leaving tiny ripples in its wake. She forgot about the cigarette; her eyes mesmerized by the fluid movements. He wore white linen trousers and a linen shirt, a satisfying contrast to his brown arms and face. Slowly, back and forth he rowed with the pool net, trapping little insects, leaves and frangipani blossoms. It was like he was performing a sacred task. She was startled when the young waitress with the shy smile placed the order down in front of her, which immediately made her foot shake again.

During the meal her eyes remained fixed on the pool cleaner. His eyes, in contrast, were half closed, repeating each movement with somnambulant care. Intermittently he took a step to the right, making his slow way around the large pool, stepping lightly over the iguanas that chewed on fallen hibiscus blossoms. She ate and drank automatically. When her plate was empty, she was surprised. She hardly ever finished her food. Stacie didn't leave until the cleaner had circled the entire pool and put down the pole. Once he'd departed, she paid and left.

Calm, refreshed and receptive she arrived in Chichen Itza, taking her time to walk around the huge archeological city of the pre-Columbian Maya civilization. On reaching the top of the Kukulkan Pyramid, or El Castillo as it's also known, she felt overawed by the view of the endless miles of jungle below her, and wanted to scream in exultation – so unlike her. Later, when she leaned against one of the columns in the Temple of a Thousand Warriors, she realized that she hadn't felt as free and enthused about anything in years. In this moment of unrepressed self-analysis, she also noted that she was perfectly content just sitting there, taking in the atmosphere and looking at people passing by. She even sat up and listened to what a tour guide had to say about the carved columns depicting images of various warriors.

Back on the highway her nervousness returned. It annoyed her that she'd only seen a small part of the huge territory and felt sick at the idea of returning to Cancun. On impulse, she put on the breaks, made a U-turn and headed back. Why not spend the night at the Kukulkan Restaurant & Bungalows?

Fifteen minutes later she'd checked into one of the cabañas. After a shower she sought out the same table under the palapa and ordered dinner. The pool cleaner was nowhere in sight. But the memory of his sacral strokes raking the pool was almost as good. That night she forgot to take the sleeping pill and slept till the sun shone through her window.

Part One

As an adamant early riser, she was astonished to note the time: 8:30, almost two hours later than usual. Not that she had anywhere particular to go. She peered out the window and saw the pool cleaner, dressed in white, already brushing off the algae from the floor with a long pool brush. His gentle but firm strokes were as even as they'd been with the skimmer net. Twenty minutes later she sat under the palapa for breakfast. Birds chirped, dew glistened on the grass, the blossoms gave off their perfume, and the gang of iguanas huddled around the pool man, who had now started to vacuum.

Systematically he moved the long aluminum pole along the bottom of the pool. His dark eyes glinted in the morning sun. Watching him was like a massage; she felt the vacuum's muzzle caress her skin, making its way along her arms, shoulders, back, belly and legs. She felt it gently loosen and suck up the debris and sediment caught on the floor of her psyche, along the sides of her mind. The pool man was thorough and he was in no hurry; time dissolved. The balanced to and fro of his rhythmic motions merged into one ongoing motif, like the throb of a jellyfish, or the gradual metamorphosis of summer clouds on a clear day. Her own body unconsciously and invisibly began to imitate the movements, her breathing leveled out, and her pulse slowed down. If the pool man noticed her staring at him, he did not show it. He kept cleaning and intermittently stepping over the stout iguanas that followed him around the pool, as if they too were in the spell of his hallowed activity.

Once he was done, Stacie returned to Chichen Itza. Before exploring she bought a guide book, determined to know all about the place that was recently named one of the new Seven Wonders of the World. The bulk of the tour busses had not yet arrived and there were many places in this expansive territory where she could be alone. The vendors were still setting up their wares along the path to the Cenote Sagrado. Stacie lingered at the impressive sinkhole, reading up on its background, imagining the nature of the sacrifices that were conducted during times of drought. She felt pity for the young girls who'd been forced to take the almost 90-foot leap to their deaths. For the rest of the morning she continued to walk through the park, feeling uncommonly tranquil, light and unburdened.

That afternoon she drove the twenty odd miles to Valladolid, bought some clothes and necessities such as toothpaste and toothbrush, and returned to Kukulkan Restaurant & Bungalows where she checked in for the rest of her stay, only to return to her hotel in Cancun the night before her scheduled departure for New York.

Every day she watched the pool man with the black hair, sun-baked skin, and white attire. Every day she let herself be massaged, brushed, caressed, sucked free of dregs and residue. Every day she felt lighter and more at peace. Every day she sensed that hardened glob in her solar plexus recede. Every day she watched, mesmerized. Every day the pool cleaner went about his business as if he never noticed her. Every day she went on little outings, ever more receptive and awake – the way she remembered herself as a teenage girl.

On the final morning, throughout the extended breakfast, she savored watching the pool man one last time – the calmness with which he went about his business. She left the pretty waitress with the shy smile a generous tip and got up to pack. She placed a second tip on top of the pool pump, wedged between the poles.

Back in New York, whenever she felt restless, impatient or annoyed, the image of the pool cleaner from the Yucatan appeared, causing her to relax and calm down almost immediately. She'd always treasure that chance meeting, though their eyes had never met.

Up in Smoke

AFTER THE ACCIDENT she left the city and moved to upstate New York, buying a small cottage at the foot of Phudd Hill, down the road from the old white house where John Cowper Powys once lived and wrote his most famous tome, *A Glastonbury Romance*. As Executive Director of ECI (Environmental Crisis Institute) that focused on grass roots works against global warming and gene technology, she had led a hectic life organizing conferences and summit meetings, filing litigations, writing articles for journals and magazines, and consulting with third world countries to develop environmental legislation, appropriate to their respective situations. She lectured widely on ecological issues and often appeared on TV, wearing her pinstriped business suit like a trademark.

Her frenetic lifestyle as one of the country's leading environmental attorneys was cut short when a semi-truck rear-ended her minivan on the Mass Pike, causing it to spin across the highway median where it was struck head-on by another vehicle. The Jaws of Life had to be used to pry her free from the car's mangled remains. She was air lifted by helicopter to Massachusetts General Hospital in critical condition, and it was 9 days before she awoke from her coma. The injuries were severe: multiple broken and fractured bones, dislocated shoulder, kidney failure, massive internal bleeding and collapsed lung. Worst of all, her left leg could not be saved and had to be amputated above the knee. Months of physical therapy followed, during which she learned how to walk with a prosthetic leg and adjust to a new reality. The long drawn out investigations into the cause of the accident eventually paid off and she won a $1, 260,000 personal injury settlement. However, it marked the end of her career at ECI.

Shortly before the accident she had received multiple death threats. She was convinced her legal victories against the chemical and biotech giant Monsanto on behalf of organic farmers had something to do with the crash, though she never voiced her suspicions. Traumatized and suffering from repeated nightmares she found solace in the country, keeping mostly to herself. The accident happened just days before her 56th birthday.

Finally, after more than a year, she began to settle into a new routine. Instead of the business suit, she now wore jeans and T-shirts, and gave up dying her hair blonde, letting the silver shine through. Every morning after breakfast, which consisted of green tea, porridge and some seasonal fruit, she went out onto the covered porch to watch the birds converge around the bird feeder, or enjoy the view across Phudd Field through which the Ockawamick Creek flowed. By 9:00 a.m. she was back inside, sitting at her desk writing rough drafts of letters, articles, reviews, editorials, critiques or commentaries on yellow notepads with an HB 2 pencil. Punctually, at 11:30 she took a coffee break, easing back on her recliner, from where she could look through the French window and delight in the constant visitation of birds. No later than noon she was at her desk again, writing. At 1:15 p.m. she put down her pencil, set aside the yellow notepad and limped down the driveway to the mail box on Harlemville Road to collect the assortment of newspapers, magazines and journals to which she subscribed – both from the right and the left of the sociopolitical landscape. She hardly ever received any personal mail, and never responded when she did.

After lunch and a catnap, she copied the letters neatly onto high quality paper with a fountain pen. With the same meticulous hand, she wrote each address, before folding and sliding the letters into matching envelopes and methodically applying the stamps. The letters were placed into a white wicker basket. The articles, however, which she revised and rewrote on her laptop, were formatted according to the specific submission guidelines of the respective magazines or journals. Once they were printed out, she put them into separate 8 ½ x 11 manila envelopes, which were put into a bigger rattan basket next to the one with the letters.

Afternoon tea (always Earl Grey) she took at 3:45 p.m., during which she paged through the newly arrived magazines, marking articles with post-its, or underlining certain sentences or paragraphs with a fine point marker – blue. In between, she opened her laptop, looked up information and made notes in an exercise book. After dinner – with pen and pad always at the ready – she watched the news channels on TV, both local and international for an hour. Sometimes, though rarely, she was drawn into watching a sitcom or a crime show, but mostly she read. At 11:00 p.m. she undressed, removed her prosthetic leg and retired to bed, where she continued to read for at least another hour before switching off the lights.

Every Monday afternoon she went to the local Farm Store in Harlemville to purchase fresh, organic or biodynamic vegetables and meats. She enjoyed these outings, chatting with the locals, especially the farmers who were struggling to survive against all odds. Nobody knew much about her, other than she was a retired attorney from the city who'd lost a leg in an unfortunate accident. She kept people at bay.

Every Saturday morning, she interrupted her usual routine to built a fire in the outdoor fireplace, where the previous owners used to enjoy their barbeques on the patio in the backyard. Once the fire was going strong, she would go back inside and gather the fruits of her week's work. With a basket in each hand she'd limp back out and place them on the stone bench in front of the fire, taking a seat between the two. For a while she would watch the flames before taking the letters and articles – one by one – and throw them into the fire. Not before each envelope was entirely burnt would she add the next one to the pyre.

The letters were mostly addressed to prominent figures in the world of science, politics, finances, culture and religion. But some letters also saluted, encouraged, and gave thanks to the efforts of individual advocates and small organizations for their persistent pursuits of justice and human dignity. Her articles served as a relentless battle against environmental threats. She'd always been good with words, using them incisively and decisively, to the dismay of her adversaries. Now her writing, more than ever, was brutally honest. She addressed every topical issue, from world hunger, sex trafficking, child labor, terrorism, right up to the latest elections. Never had her words been as piercing and to the point.

Every week she watched her work burn. Nothing ever deterred her. In the thick of winter, when it was too cold or snowy to step outside, she continued her ritual in front of the blazing wood stove. Every Saturday, without fail, she fed her thoughts to the flames, effecting change, their messages dispersing throughout the world like a delicate, rarefied dye in the sky. Every Saturday, with a slight smile hovering in the corners of her mouth, her neatly inked thoughts went up in smoke, disseminating homeopathically across the globe.

Optimistic Freshman

CHARLES MUSGRAVE got shot in the shoulder. Though the bullet shattered his collarbone, he didn't complain and insisted that the guy who shot him was a real gentleman and had no intention of hurting him. We all knew better.

Bad luck followed Charles wherever he went, like flapping vultures after road kill. Hardly a week went by without some mishap or calamitous event. But he remained upbeat and his perpetual smile was infectious. As his teacher, I could never get angry at him, though he hardly ever did his homework, was easily distracted, and chatted incessantly. He was the most picked on freshman in our entire high school. Halfway through the year the seniors had already nominated him for the runt of the year award. A week after getting shot, his mother died of AIDS. I went to the funeral, a cold and overcast day in mid-January.

His father arrived in shackles, escorted by two guards. He was serving time for voluntary manslaughter and wouldn't be out for years. Hampered by his leg irons, he shuffled toward the dozen or so freezing people gathered sullenly around the open grave, coming to a clinking stop next to Charles. His orange jumpsuit stood out against the drab cluster of black-clad mourners and bare trees. Charles's uncle, playing priest, mumbled a few perfunctory parting words. Some tears were shed, followed by fistfuls of dirt that hit the slipshod coffin like hard hail against a corrugated roof.

His father was denied permission to attend the reception, which was anyway nothing more than a coffee-and-pie-deal at a nearby diner. Charles shrugged it off, smiling as usual. "I'm just glad my Dad could come to the funeral. It doesn't usually happen. He really loved my mother." We knew better. We also knew that Charles was now the sole provider for his younger brother and sister, though he insisted that his uncle and aunt would help. But they were too stoned or drunk most of the time and could barely help themselves.

Before leaving the reception, I told him about an early pilgrim I'd recently read about, who also went by the name of Charles Musgrave — a puritan who'd emigrated to America in the early 1620s. Apparently, he was so excited to see the New World's sandy shores that he fell overboard and drowned.

Charles clasped his hands together in a revelatory manner, sighed and said, "Ah, so it's all in the name, huh?" Moments later he chuckled, slurped down the last sip of coffee and said, "Hey, maybe people should just call me Dick."

Charles Musgrave dropped out of school a couple of days later.

Yeah, I Killed My Girlfriend

KEN ENTERED our educational treatment center for at-risk youth after serving three years in a maximum-security juvenile facility for murdering his girlfriend at age twelve, though in the end it was ruled a homicide. Lucky for him he'd been tried as a minor and released early to us for good behavior and a vehement desire to study and change his ways.

Now, at fifteen he was a looming 6' 8" – the proverbial gentle giant with a friendly smile and soft, sonorous voice. Even when he was first arrested, he'd stood 6' 2" tall. His transcripts also stated that when he entered the juvenile institution, he had a wild temper, but that he calmed down soon enough when he got acquainted with his new surroundings and was no longer exposed to drugs. The only recorded infraction during his stint at the detention and reform facility told of an incident that occurred between him and a senior juvie who'd dropped the n-word and falsely accused him of hogging contraband. One punch and the foolish bully landed in the infirmary with a broken jaw. From then on, the correctional officers often encouraged him to help keep the youths from fighting, which he did if it was justified and would keep his friends from any further unnecessary penalties.

During the year he spent with us he continued his new found passion for bench pressing, reading and studying. He could already bench over 350 pounds. As his case manager I saw his potential and was determined to help ease his way back into the community. A relationship of trust developed between us and over time I also found myself calling on him to help sort out arguments between some of the other delinquent students. He had a gift for finding the right words to resolve arguments, and when the need arose, he used his muscle power to stop fights. Nobody dared to stand up against Ken, not only because of his intimidating physique, but because he'd gained everybody's respect. I felt good about writing him a favorable recommendation for a prestigious high-end school from which he hoped to graduate with a 4.0. He had the smarts to match his solid 260-pound frame. After he received the long-awaited acceptance letter, he came to visit me in my office one last time.

"Yeah, I killed my girlfriend," he said after a few minutes of friendly banter, "but it was an accident... an accident, you hear what I'm sayin'?" His usual smile faded and he looked stern. "I came to tell you that. They accused me wrong. It was no murder. I was loading my 9 mm Luger, yeah, stolen, when it went off. Don't know how it happened. I shoulda been more careful, but I was high on meth at the time. Anyway, I got such a fright that I pulled the trigger again... shot her two more times." Two tears rolled down his smooth black cheeks. "I loved her like a sista, you feel me? She cared for me when my Mom was on crack and my Dad... well, you know...I had many dads – all duds. But what was I gonna do, me, a black kid from the streets of Harlem? The public defender told me to plead guilty, you know, in exchange for a lenient plea bargain. So I did, and I guess it's served me well, because it got me off the streets and gave me another chance – but I didn't murder her!"

Ken broke out in a sweat, and because it was obvious that he was reliving a painful memory, I interrupted him, saying it's all water under the bridge and that he should forget the past and focus on the future. Instead, he lifted his two large hands as if he was preparing to spar, shook his head and shouted, "No, hear me out!" He paused, dropped his clenched fists, sighed, and continued in a lowered voice. "Sorry, man, but here's the thing – I gotta tell you... gotta tell someone." His eyes darted around while he blinked repeatedly. He coughed to clear his throat. "Thing is, I killed two other guys for which I was never caught." Ken looked me straight in the face, gauging my reaction. "Yeah, I was angry, but I knew what I was doing when I shot them. But my girlfriend... that was an accident!"

Part One

He got up, breaking out in a smile, and shook my hand like he was shooing off a swarm of pesky wasps. "Figured you had to know... you've done so much for me. I trust you." I kept mum about his admission, though by law I was required to report him.

Two years later I received a card from him letting me know that he'd graduated with honors and that he was thinking of moving out west. For twelve years I heard no more from him till last week when I received a manila envelope from Missouri. It contained a newspaper cutting about a "Hero Priest" who'd risked his life running into a burning house and saving two children. In the photo that accompanied the article I recognized an older, but still smiling Ken, shaking the Fire Chief's hand. In the paper's margin, scribbled in red pen, were the words: *Every Sunday when I give my sermon, I think of you. Two down and one to go – know what I mean? God bless, Ken*

4'33"

In honor of John Cage's centennial 1912 – 1992

HE CLIMBED up the stairs and said – NO MORE. Sinking into the sofa he wired himself to his iPod, thumbed for the track 4'33" of silence, shut his eyes and listened. Within a minute he pulled out the white ear buds and shifted over to the piano, determined to play the entire piece himself – all three movements.

Palpitations punched against unwelcome thoughts during the first 30 seconds. Toward the end of the 2' 23" middle movement his breathing and pulse steadied and he surfed through a lapis lazuli tunnel. The illusory peace parted in the last 40 seconds, when graphic images of his flame-turn-femme-fatale sucked him into Charybdis' gullet, spitting him out in gut-grime rage.

Foiled, he slammed the piano lid shut, jumped up and kicked the stepladder that led to the attic where he hid his past and kept his future caged. The rickety ladder crashed onto his guitar. With a yelp he snatched his old Epiphone and sat on the sofa to inspect – JUST A MINOR DENT, NO CRACKS. Relieved, he again set the timer of his iPod stopwatch.

Hugging his guitar, he settled into silence, this time playing it as one instead of three movements. EVERYBODY NEEDS THEIR 4'33" OF SILENCE, he thought – A TIME TO REACH OUT INTO A FREED SPACE OF NOTHING. Halfway through his cell phone erupted with Radiohead's "Creep" ringtone. Unable to ignore the techno-nymph he put his six strings back on the stand and silenced his cell, growling at the unwanted caller – the one he'd love

Part One

to stick in the attic and stuff into a box, together with all the diaries, letters, photos and vinyl albums.

Walking over to the French window, he blew a vapor heart on the glass, and cut a cross through it with his tongue. The cold of the pane calmed him. CAN'T BE THAT DIFFICULT, he thought. LET'S TRY DRUMMING. He set the timer for a third attempt, jammed his djembe between his knees and began.

After seven seconds Merce, his beagle, scratched against the front door, needing to pee in the garden; the squirrel with the split ear started raiding the bird feeder; and after 2'54" he suddenly remembered the appointment he should be at. From nowhere a great line for a poem flashed up which would evaporate if he didn't write it down immediately; thick raindrops plodded on the deck, and the washing needed to be brought in.

Undeterred he played on, drumming in perfect silence, eyes closed, accepting the moment and its peripheral sounds, letting them go – letting it all go, releasing his remorse and freeing his fears, his need to control. He forgave her and wrapped her up in his warm hush. All sounds ceased. He'd made it through the 4'33". Space was transformed and stillness resounded. IT NEEDS PRACTICE — DAILY. He felt un-caged.

Fringe Location

Mystical night toward the end of Apartheid, Grahamstown, South Africa – Dedicated to Keith

KEITH SAT ENSCONCED in an old off-white wicker chair, a book on his lap, left barefoot leg up on the coffee table, eyes staring at the faded floral wallpaper in front of him, while his right hand unconsciously caressed the wicker weave. In between he looked down, read a couple of sentences before losing himself in the patterned hydrangeas once more. He breathed deeply, sighed, got up, shoved the book back into the rickety bookshelf amongst the others, and desultorily moved his fingertips across the spines from right to left, mouthing fragments of the titles. He scratched his beard, walked over to the fridge, and tugged at the door. It released a squelchy squeal as it grudgingly opened. He gazed into the flickering cavernous innards. After an elongated pause he shoved the door shut with a pneumatic thud. Keith yawned softly, stretched and trudged over to the window. He pushed the lace curtains aside and glanced up at the six-day old moon. That's when his head shook like a dog shaking off water and his eyes took on a glint.

Slap my thighs, tug at my beard, huh! What's this – capitulating to deadening inertia? Out with it, man, you slob-gut-pudding of the earth, put a match to your movements. Flex your limbs and cough away that gruff catarrh. I hear you, Lady Moon, tantalizing me with

Part One

your nubile profile, gazing into the distance with pointy peaks, veiled in silver saliva. *Aikhona*! This mantic night shines hooping beams inside my churning belly. Unfetter this phlegma and pounce into the night with spinal energies. Get off your *agtergat* and *jol* through the streets of Grahamstown. See what you can find.

Come sandals, my trusty *tire-tekkies*, testaments of destiny – you who secure each fragmentary step as I slap, whack, and stealthily stroke the pavements, gravel tracks, game trails, tarmac highways, thorn-filled veld, dew-pearled meadows, or sand-stretched beaches. Be now – once again – my glinting eyeballs, my cupped ears to the ground, so that I may walk and dance to red earth's rhythms, following the *spoors* to who knows what. I will become a slinking truth-sleuth, to harpoon the fruits of darkness, stepwise, as I crunch explosive potential. I'll be a roaming detonator, igniting thought-bolts with each onward stride.

Bare little room, you cannot confine me. Not tonight, for sure. Puny lightbulb hanging limp from the ceiling, your feeble sheen is a pathetic tear of despair. These staid walls are no place for me right now. No, I'll catch and scoop up my squawking savage energy, wring its neck, let a rush of gold pulse from my formidable ancestry, and drink its alchemical draft. Now, get the hell out of this dank den to taste and penetrate this fecund night's loins.

A chilly night in mid-June, though the earth whispers sultry from the shadows and through my antenna toes – something you'd know nothing about, privileged burghers of Grahamstown, safely lodged behind your gated abodes, fortified walls, solidly barred windows. You live lily-sweet on borrowed time. Tell me, proud burghers, when are you going to cut the chords of your tenuous power? Your streets are empty. I look up at your curtained windows, lights shutting off, one by sporadic one, some giving off the lonely blue tint of your TV dreams. You'll all go to sleep soon, though you've been sleeping for years; yet the question remains: When will you awake? When will you have the courage to cross over fear's threshold – to sniff pellucid air, exonerate yourself from disdainful repressions, and expand your chests with life's wind-spirit? I dare you to let yourselves be dislodged and enter the vital emptiness with trust! You'd locate the unexpected and find yourselves thriving on the jiving surprises that are always on the creative loose. There's time yet to join the dance of the nimble mind, to discover the communal hug of souls, and be gifted with swelling senses, while your body builds willful contact. Kick a stone, change life. Take a spill into the open. Free yourselves from your burgher bedrooms, dull dining, languid living rooms. Strike dead flint and create sparks. Paint yourself a memory. Forget your mastery that gives you spurious security. Be a sister and discover how many siblings you have; how many you've never met? Be a brother.

Ah-ha, you were bound to appear, displaced Cathedral, relic of centuries past, burdened with tradition. You still stand tall in phallic silence, your bodyguard trees whispering and exposing your slanders. Do you hear them, do you perceive the echo of your own heretical talk, or, to be more precise, the heresies proclaimed within your noble structure? They could be a sonic mirror to your hearts, if only you'd listen. You'd perceive dissenting babble. Listen, the trees have more to tell, as does the bushveld and the stellar *sterre* above: truths to make the Saints – the selfless ones – push back their halos in humble gratitude, those lucky enough to have been privy to the fragments of their exclusive songs. Become exclusive – you indolent burghers – before you exclude yourselves. Do you even know the *preter*-significance of the archangel and his temporal counterpart after whom you're named? Cathedral of St. Michael and St. George, the macro- and microcosmic Saints battling against injustice, inequality, and all that leads to these iniquities: the dragon. Trees cannot be silenced if the wind, the gentle zephyr, comes to visit bearing its story. The wind cannot be ordered mute nor forever cornered.

Looming Cathedral, your frigid portals are locked. How do you breathe? Blow those demon bundles away, those that mockingly reside on your altar, masturbating and sodomizing, wielding dildo candles, waxen erections – ignoble scions of lies, greed and *isms*. No Sunday perfume will exorcise these enslaved puppets. Yet, risky life remains, evident in the cheesy squeaks of young church mice, recurrently chased by the watchful cat in residence. Survival in the woods of organ pipes and bellows is an art. To pull at the registers fills tubular trees, the hard-pressed keys unlocking volumes of wind, causing spiders to lose their webs, falling wispily across pulpit and faithful pews, while the glass-stained windows come close to shattering – a bowel bubble of wind held tight within the pressed cheeks of dogmatism. Cathedral, make room for fresh winds to induce your catharsis. Alas, for now it's fated to lie as nightmares within the seams of your gothic walls, muttered abroad in codes of bat wings or furtively flashing signals around the steeples, towers, lesser spires – blind flights – one day to be metamorphosed into turtle doves, melodies to the harmonic drone of wind washed trees: holy invisibles, Africa's ancestors, merging with Madonna earth, accompanied by hordes of holy aliens.

But who *is* the Alien? The repugnant man-nation who has outgrown the measured cut-of-the norm's groove (the oppressors' determinations) or those still unborn? We're all Aliens of sorts. A relief to know that most Saints were sinners whose afflictions were hot coals across which they stepped – their wills unscathed – to transport themselves to loftier levels in the fulfilment of needs, inviting wayfarers and *waysiders* to join the march, dropping coins of selflessness along the road to Purgation. Who is the Alien? Is it I or the cumulation of this alarm-locked town? And who are the exiled? The ones whose ancestors wetted Africa's earth for thousands of years? Finding one's identity has many levels, and can only be found if we live into the *I-dentity* of others.

My loneliness is attached to the stars and to the worms that enrich the soil; the humble and the grand – swayed between their shifting magnitude. And yours, white burghers – have you tapped it yet? Is it found in the plug which offers electro-magnetic opportunities to straightjacket yourselves within the color oceans of TV screens and quadrophonic extravaganzas? Or the sunny Sunday gatherings around the grill, the *braaivleis* munch and chew of your tenuous privilege? Or maybe the unacknowledged taste of forbidden guilt, stored in your camel's humps, persisting to push-squeeze it through the needle hole of your lucky minority? Through the color of my skin I am part of you. There's time yet to become holy. But we have to act, though I fear it's too late. Though we'll fail, we have to try. It means becoming Alien, that is: Of the New.

Hey Eric, my *boetie* on the far side of the world; I call on you, your spirit, to rise forth and merge with mine, to become part of this nocturnal emulation of relinquished light. Hey, *chommie*, thwack the dust and sand from your blues harp – you solitary expatriate – and wail some raunchy blues profusions into the night air and join me in my foot-stomping-soul-flinging rambles through this deserted ghost town. But I guess your monk bare feet are taking you down your own dark-aged cobbly alleys while mustering up against your own madness, looking for writings on the wall, a Madonna to harbor you in her open lap with wine, bread and blessings. Let's pump hands across the oceans. We'll lead each other on, the pilgrimage of the unshod spirit-*Mensch*, always forwards on the road, ever and forever; the two of us, kindred Aliens. We'll weep sweat, cry nectar, excrete holy manure in reverential exchange for terrestrial intimacies, making allowances for each in morphological abandonment to steer future-wise this earthly seedling ship. We'll trail in the wake of angels, the gods. Hail to you, veritable guides, you who dig your wings deep into the earth of our changing failures, offering your efforts for our struggling stripling attempts to conquer our doom in this human trauma. Hey-ho, we won't fail you in the long run, to hallow this ground beneath our bony and calloused feet, we'll not let ourselves succumb into a hodgepodge of rot in the crown of the firmament.

S'truths, as I trample along this trammeled town I vow to you mother Africa – great *Unkulunkulu* – that I will cast my fire-willed body with all my potent might into your curdling oceans, labial mellow gorges, cliff-jaw'd mountains, the rugged-belly-*veld*-expanses, my schnoz into the fuming armpits of your ghettos and cities, my inner ear diffusions fondling myriad timbres of your scooping blood-pumped voice – the guttural purrs and chants from throat depths to the ecstatic ululations, the hissing of wangling snakes, while our tongues taste the salt bitter freshness of your wide-warm pans and dimpled moss-cool pools. And with my preternatural urgings of gushing sensuality I will engender your cervices with sea-man semen love, becoming one with the fundamentals, propagating irredeemable undercurrents of spirit magnanimity. No water, be it in the lagoons, dams, taps, reservoirs, or calabashes will be left untouched from my injected *muthi,* baptismal blessings. No airy breath shall be without catalytic exhalation of devotion. Each bite transmuted into bolus will exude the life song of mental transubstantiation, adjoining the mint of selflessness. All nourishments ravished, the simplest victuals utterly destroyed and resurrected through the force of mystic anabolism – the rapturous assimilation of life substances, metamorphosed. Thus, the separated shall be joined, each to each. Compassion, like blood, birthed in marrow, will transfuse and flow through all of humanity, and ultimately reign for the peace of all for all, the great reintegration – the poison of worldly Apartheid – sad segregation – eradicated, for good. This is my promise, my vow, my oath. And allied souls will join to enlighten this moment, to pursue the lust to beget new life into this, our ill-ageing earth, to form eurythmic processions, chanting litanies that diffuse into the world ether, forming a filmy chrysalis, one day to burst, tremoring the starry spheres, causing the zodiac to rumble awake from its dormant state in our fortified hearts, the Logos having created an independence of creation, interdependent and freed through love. *Ubuntu*!

Dinkum, my soles are touching tar, padding along, a stranger to this town, but not to this earth, because I'm a native of the African *krantz, koppie, donga,* and lush lagoons dozing in latent might. Darkness all around. I ask you: where do my *fountainous* thoughts shoot from? Darkness, are you a source, the womb of inner light? I am ignorant of your domain's dimensions. Your veil conveys covered messages from sense-free invisibles. Unseen, untamed spirits speak from every brook, pebble, and *gogga.* Your *tokoloshes* come to warn us. Are you the seething sap to pry or massage open the fiery petals of my shadow-chakras – to let raw energy rage throughout my body and mind in uproarious delight? On what substance do you feed? Where lie your frontiers when mere imaginations sling forth and give vent to inspirations, intuitions? Am I being fooled, tested? Or are these steadfast expressions of truth? What visions do you procure-secure to make prophets of us – or only to ourselves for a fractional night. Why tonight? Now? Who holds the gravity of your prime note? What battles have been waged to see you naked? Is guiltless nudity an ultimatum, a forbidden fruit, or the reward for deeds done, mere grace? Does it hide illusions or is it the dress of humiliation? Thoughts, you enter me. In my hubris I always thought I created you. The hubris of our age. The hubris that feeds greed, the insatiable ego.

Thought sources abound. Each vernal spring is a being, though not all are benevolent. Must learn to discern. The uterus-mind conceives according to love, temptations, or indolence. I see that now. Thoughts of widening warmth – do not let it burn you. Thoughts of mechanical cold – do not let it freeze you. Two evils. Balance – must hold sway. I'd hail such a long-awaited being? To partner with this power, which is as gentle as a lover's touch, a woman's sacrifice – as she offers her breast to her babe. To have *Balance* in the heart's purse, to see diffusing equalities, to have the capacity to order our thoughts, the way blood is controlled in its circulatory system in constant rhythmic renewal. Thoughts: All comprehensive in *one* – a culmination of gods, manifested in the *twinning* of freedom and love, the *trinity* of Beauty, Goodness, and Truth; in the *quartet* of North, South, East, West; in the human *pentagram* of Spirit, Fire, Air, Water, and Earth; in the *hexagram* of the Star of David: two triangles merging into one – the above and below – macrocosm and microcosm; in the *heptagram* of the seven planets; and finally, the holy *twelve* that is the *zodiac* that is the peripheral-centripetal emanation that is the all-encompassing one – the unity, which revolves and returns to sun love – the eternal *Ubuntu*.

And thus accompanied, I drive you along the innermost gullet of my selfhood to be purged in the combustion of my passioned

Part One

strivings, warmed into soothing secretions, to heal the slave-wounds of the world, one at a time. Thought, it is you who must lift the riddling lid to the puzzle-box, you who must spin questions into answers, annulling the need to fall into the vacuum. Through hearts' equilibrium, belief will turn to trust in the workings of gradual growth. Grit of the *earth*, I hereby declare that I *do* now understand you as an initial and living thought, which is a vision, to grate the souls of humans to advance, to cultivate the senses in acute obedience to the ever-changing arrival of life. And further, to absorb it in its entirety, its core, where it may meet its own membership in its earthly saga. Pulsating thought is the song of the word, the start of the call, the great-all re-call; even you, shoe shop; or you, pharmacy, hardware store, grocer. Yes, thoughts made you. They'll lead you if you heed them.

I pause in my wild perambulations and return to the original thought of the earth before it became an assemblage of matter, a manifestation of primal motivation. And I marvel, as I marvel at the thought of humans before there was clay. But now as I gawk and gaze at those blond and afro-wigged mannequins in the stores, or the electric shavers, sunglasses, jackets, ties, dresses, shawls, shirts, and other dummy temptations, I feel my thoughts knocking against an anonymous state, and my mind listens to the threatened existence. Strange window shopper that I am on this *med-way* night, traipsing through this emptied Grey-hams-town at this late hour. Doubt indents my mind as to how noble and dignified we have made use of all the thought-multitudes available to us – segregating the daily bread of life. I throw out my net and haul in the catch, letting them meld in my mind's melting pot, to form ingots, worthy to be utilized in the commerce of worldly affairs, forged into sharp swords to pierce through the adamant muck of accumulated thoughtlessness, to reach the nether caverns through which the Western dragon crawls – wherein to chain him, word for word, link for link.

I resume my peripatetic monologue, but my footsteps grow heavy. My thoughts fade and my feelings have lost their flames, have turned into embers. My weighty limbs pull at my head. I sense the turgid thuds of my mingled blood trudging along its cyclic course. My deliberations are like fruit turned *vrot*. My awareness is fermenting, or have I been subject to its billowing fancies all along. Why so short lived, these mystic flashes that feel like inspirations, allowing me to peek behind the façade of matter, of *Natura* in her temporal form. The pain of mortality is the inevitable loss of *Euphorion*, only moments after birthing that new life with its instantaneous insights. Scattered thrill-thoughts, hallowed feelings, adrenalin pumped muscles, where have you gone? Have you ceased to be, or do you have a life of your own – moved on like capricious wafts? Or was it just figments of my tropical emotions.

I'm exhausted: a stale dull animal treading the blue globe; a dethroned mammal, cartoon of a human being. And only a minute ago I was a supra-child, released and interconnected, feeling the flow through an opened fontanel, an ecstasy, proving my higher source. Sleep, slice of daily death, the other realm to calm and digest the wakeful hours. On these deserted streets, paradoxically enough, I feel the peace such rest can bring – a homeland for all living creatures, where segregation becomes meaningless.

Can't delude myself; it is loneliness I now bear. The manacles of physical denseness have got me again in their talon grasp. Heaven and earth, with you I can commune, but from my neighbors I'm cut off by impenetrable psychic barriers, built and forged through cultural and political constructs. These shut-shops, conveying sterility, neon nullity, telling me of my outcast nature. *Opskud!* Keep walking off towards the outskirts. Must load up on a gut-full of starry inhalations, must add fuel to the embers, connect those fine strands again, those that had initially occasioned me to bound out into the night with such abandon.

Wider and longer than I thought, these streets. But lofty sister Moon-horn, thank you for your monthly spilt milk wisdom! How do you cope with your melancholic dislocation? Share this loneliness with me tonight. How long will my dislodgement last? Tell me about your reflective nature. How does it feel to redirect the sun and not have a source of light within you? I want my own light, it's what I seek, but, unlike you, my constant reflections confuse me, though I know it's what I need to get me out of this maze I find myself in. Maybe my mirror is too warped and I must find ways to flatten it. Prick open, milky moon, the metal finish on my looking glass with the sharpness of your pointy cusps, so that I can behold the true semblance of the stars, that ghost of Humanity Yet to Come. Me, the synthesis of the firmament, though reduced to a mite in a constellation of dust. Then why do I intermittently feel myself in symbiosis with the spangled firmament, warmed through with sun-dust – a minute confluence of the molten macro substance?

Breezy sweet air, my skin you touch, my lungs you fill. I savor your concern. How many lovers have you had? None and all? All *one* to you! A vestal windy virgin, messaging secrets. You puff the shape of loneliness into a dress of fragrant sadness, laced with parting comfort, leaving me to my own momentary existence on this singular June night, with a nascent chill in the air. Why do I shiver? Is it the cold or the moon's aloofness?

The hard asphalt sidewalk tugs at my head, bends my back. My eyes roam through the blackness – shuts me up.

Forty yards in front of Keith, lodged between sprawling oak trees, a large group of Africans occupied the pavement and the embankment beyond. He'd been so preoccupied he hadn't noticed them. Many sat in the shadows or were huddled around old oil drums, warming themselves, the red-hot coals glowing through the air holes. Others leaned against the tree trunks. Looming shadows undulated all along the pavement.

Immediately, out of an inner reflex, he thought to cross the road to the other side – to avoid confrontation. A flotsam of thoughts flashed through his mind: *Apartheid – Black Resistance – Terrorism – Freedom Fighters – Communism – Banning…* Already his feet had stumbled off the pavement… *Trials – ANC – Torture – Interrogations*

– Detentions – Massacres – Raids… More headlines came to mind: *Steve Biko Murdered – Sharpville Holocaust – 76 July Riots – Upheavals – Riots in Soweto – Location Fingo Village – Grahamstown's Protest: focal point!* Unwittingly, he'd walked toward Fingo Village.

The far side of the road was empty. Instinctually, his limbs wanted to cross the road to escape the precarious situation. *What a typically white thing to do, to cross the road like a cowering dog caught crapping*, he thought to himself, knowing he'd been seen. "Where's my trust," he hissed to himself. "Hell, I will continue, I'll show my solidarity with their cause." Keith had participated in the July riots of 76, and was an outspoken activist against Apartheid. Disgusted at himself for almost crossing the road, exposing his fragility and guilt, he stepped back onto the pavement. It had only been a matter of seconds – his vulnerable wavering – but it remained freeze-framed in his mind. Tense, but with resolve, he approached their domain of choice (in violation of curfew laws), noticing even more figures shuffling within the shadows of a tall stone wall.

The winds lifted and rustled through the dried oak leaves above him. Firmly, he strode into the crowd, the soft swells of chanting women, the low syncopated hum of men – earthy and full – a smoldering presence of smoke, sweat and purpose. Muffled drum palpitations carried the dense and laden current onwards like slow-motion cloud-scapes across the vast semi-arid deserts, with intimations of flash floods tonguing along dry river beds. Some women swayed, immersed within the untrammeled incantations of time. Out of an intuitive sign of respect he relaxed his pace, matching his steps to the rhythm of the muted music, so as not to transgress into their hour of holy *indaba*; an inner territory – a fringe location, unobtainable to the power-laws of white-dominance. He could relate to their slow brewing resistance, their attempt to free the fettered spirits from the clutches of socio-political imperialism. He understood this temporary resettlement, the ineffable region between the beats, joined, as they were, by the tens of thousands of impis killed in battles, the sufferings of the 'coloured' castaways throughout the centuries. The potency of the beyond was visceral.

Part One

It seeped into him and his heart filled with empathy. In this hovering moment, Keith united with these African emancipators – supplicants of freedom, exemplars of the struggle to transform Apartheid into *Togetherheid,* based not only on mutual respect, but understanding and love for each other's respective cultures and what each can gift to the other. Keith, who breathed the soul and spirit of the African soil with elemental intimacy, felt both his difference and connectedness to them, his fellow humans – sharing the path to freedom, but with different obstacles.

He looked over at the babies asleep on their mothers' backs, wrapped tightly in blankets, and he envisioned a new future for them. *They deserve a different South Africa. That innocent security they now feel, needs to extend into the long line of tomorrows. But what awaits them? Their fathers' lost battles, life of oppression and servitude?* Compassion for this roofless hamlet overwhelmed Keith, dissolving the last vestiges of fear. He saw their strength, heard their power in their chanting and drumming, thud for persevering thud, carried by the unerring rhythms of life, which, in time, would wear down the desperate attempts to keep the keen nations shut off and separated in pens, locations, homelands, reservations.

"Take me," he thought, his lips mouthing the words. "I give myself to you in humility. Pour libations with my blood, if it may redeem some of the pain my race has made and caused you to suffer." His eyes spoke as much – the spontaneous authentic missive.

Lifting his arm, he greeted the congregation, his eyes fanning around for all to read. From the dark hollows he absorbed the glistening faces, though they remained withdrawn, distant. As he entered their space, the drumming and singing diminished, then ceased. Only the membranous hum and hush of the thickset trees persisted – the sturdy oaks, solidly set in the pavement, the roots digging deep into the earth, the thick curvaceous branches hanging over the street, the sibilant rustlings of the dried leaves tremoring intermittently.

Keith, with each tread, searched for recognition, something to hold on to. The melded moment swelled as the moving shadows remained noncommittal. Out of the suspended silence, from deep within the hidden vibrancy, came a set of answering eyes that held onto Keith's gaze with arcane penetration – the ostensible leader of them all. Keith came to a stop in front of him, this man who commanded instant and paramount respect, who was more like an *Inyanga* than a chief – a healer of people, a diviner, an elder, chosen to lead his people to freedom. As Keith stood in silent expectation in front of this tall muscled man, he realized why and what had initiated him to issue out into this partly moonlit night with such uncanny momentum: it was for *this* moment, *this* meeting. In this epiphanic instant he not only understood, but experienced the full meaning of *UBUNTU – I am because we are – the universal human bond that we all share.* In a tone that reached up from ancestral realms, though awake with political acumen, this *umfundisi*, this leader, lit up by the light of the glowing coals in the large oil drum, greeted Keith: "Goodnight, *boetie.*" He lifted his *knobkerrie,* waving it in a slow wide arc, opening the way for Keith to pass through, adding, "*Hamba Gahle* – go well, *Nkosi.*"

"*Sala Gahle* – stay well, *Sangoma.*"

PART TWO

NON-FICTION

Draft Dodger

THE DAY I RECEIVED my call up papers – in the form of a thin brown envelope – requesting my military services, I knew I wouldn't go: *No bloody way. I'd rather leave South Africa than fight for a white supremacist government. That'll be the day.* I'd sort something out. Apply for an extension. Continue my studies.

For the most part I was a confirmed pacifist, though the fighter in me was alive and well. I could identify with Achille's anger, but violence, the way it lived in the world, I abhorred. South Africa, Africa as such, is a breeding place for violence – untamed, elemental violence. It lurks around every moment's corner. You're braced for it on a semiconscious level. I had eluded it – somehow – though caught within its magnetic field all too often. Luck, chance, grace?

Violence: part of the territory, a continental theme reaching back to antediluvian times. Violence embodied in nature – the vengeful voice of the supernatural, the untrammeled rage of the eternal spirits, gods and goddesses, ancestors, myriad primal beings behind and within *Natura's* ever-changing apparel. The living elements in dire battle with one another. I bore witness to it: droughts – sun sizzling down with merciless vigor; flash floods – filling up dried river beds and farmlands and pans and entire valleys, within minutes/seconds; fires – scorching and burning everything in sight; storms – with tempestuous fury, fiercely scouring and spreading their havoc with intense acrimony, nature's cacophonous curse. Violence, violence, unadulterated violence, erupting from the depths of the earth – particles of revenge in each grit of grainy dust. A land raped, mutilated and discarded: *dongas*, deserts, mine dumps, ghettos – all wounds, scars and scabs, blemishing the once so supple and sensuous body.

Part Two

And the ravishing continues, as if she hasn't been harassed, abused, exploited enough. Violence, Africa's deadly narcotic, imbibed from birth, leaving people benighted for the lack of an antidote, for the lack of help, of love. Tribe against tribe; race against race; factions against factions; ideologies in constant conflict; rich against poor; powerful against the weak; the oppressed against the suppressers – one against the other. Blood against blood, for blood. Skirmishes, warfare, genocide, enslavement. And all feeding on *fear* and *power*, that cold current ceaselessly shocking people into randomly vile actions, spilling the red milk of humanity, dappled with leaden tears, fraught with salty sorrow. Violence, not to be ignored, its real source buried alive under the heavy red earth of denial.

Africa's hope lies in its capacity to endure; to act out of its greatest virtue – patience.

I saw violence festering, locked within the fierce laws of Apartheid. Though, it is true, I was caught up in my own subjective world all too often – the flimsily safe world of white suburbia – I couldn't ignore it. It was too much in my face. Daily I observed dastardly and humiliating occurrences – every park bench screaming with injustice, the depth of the divide, with its *white* or *non-white* signs branding the eyes. The iniquity of the vile system visible in the eyes of every black African, Indian, Chinese, Japanese (considered 'honorary' whites – what kind of honor is that?), Bushman – the veritable and tragically hounded San people, and the so called 'Coloureds.' As long as the gulf between the people cannot be bridged, violence will thrive, to this day and beyond – Africa's 'continental divide.' Without at least a combined attempt to bridge the differences . . . *Africa Addio!*

Yes, on the surface I was a pacifist, but in the vile face of apartheid I felt shots of violence injected into my system, all but drowning the lamb within me. How could anybody observe the constant practices of injustice and do nothing about it? It made me want to destroy, to grab sticks of dynamite, hand grenades, bombs – anything – and blow up all and everything that had to do with the *system*. Instead, I funneled my aggression into pen and paper, guitar and piano, transforming the soul-magma into song and music – exemplars of protest, but I just came across as the angry young man, making people feel uncomfortable. The trivial acoustic guitar and the tinkling piano strings were, however, not enough to convey my sentiments. I wanted more. Something Promethean. Something akin to the power of rock, to express what I felt. *Beethovian.*

At the height of the July riots of 76 (after 114 children had been killed by the anti-riot squad) I took part in the demonstrations organized by Wits students. Friends and I climbed up the fire escape to the top of a high-rise building adjacent to Wits University. Thousands stood gathered below, demonstrating against the education imposed on Black South Africans by the government. Alone the *idea* that they should be taught and instructed in Afrikaans – the language of the oppressors – was preposterous. Traffic on Jan Smuts Avenue had come to a complete halt, and police were everywhere. Wits' students were out in full force, showing their affiliation to the African youth, demonstrating their outrage at those killed by the police. We held up a large bedsheet on which we'd painted our slogans. A gust of wind almost sent us plummeting into the crowd below while we stood close to the edge, spreading out the sheet like a sail. We screamed our words of defiance to the thousands below. Our words of *"Amandla!* (Power), and *"One Azania, one Nation!"* got lost in the wind, but we were making a statement, expressing our solidarity with the blacks – their struggle. It didn't take long for security to arrive, who ordered us away.

The day finally arrived – my last on African soil. January 4th – call up day for hundreds of young white South African males, me included. My exemption had been unequivocally denied. And attempts to leave the country at an earlier date had failed. Eleventh hour departure.

Yet, I felt compelled to pursue one last hurrah. Though frantic and on edge, with so much still left undone, I couldn't resist the idea of hearing my name called out, only to turn my back on the military establishment and walk leisurely away. It seemed like such an enticingly 'up yours' kind of thing to do; as if by doing so, I could immortalize this turning point in my life. In my small way I was showing them that – yes – I could beat the system; I, little David, could face up to big guy Goliath and escape his clumsy clutches. More than that, I was trying to prove something to myself: I was seizing the moment, savoring the knowledge that, finally, I was taking hold of my independence – beholden to nobody. I fancied that it must be like listening to your own death sentence, then stepping away – alive. Maybe it was just a manifestation of my eccentricity, some false vanity, or just the poet in me, seeking a novel moment. Whatever the motivation, I was determined to witness my call up moment.

The big and strangely subdued crowd gathered and grew on the huge parking lot above Milner Park. The dull overcast morning was tense with prickly apprehension. Families and girlfriends had come to see the new recruits off, trying to prolong the last few minutes before the age-old battle-Moloch would intervene. Army vehicles stood around with ominous severity, in vaguely organized clusters, ready to take truckloads of us off to stipulated camps. A megaphoned uniform climbed onto the back of one of the green trucks, lists in hand, and began shouting out the names of the respective servicemen. I stood at the outer rim of the sullen assemblage, conscious of my mounting unease. What if someone should discover me? No joke then. I wondered if it wasn't in my best interest to just quietly remove myself, now, before it's too late. Why, after all, provoke fate? But I was rooted to the spot, hiding behind long hair, tipping the rim of my straw hat lower down over my forehead.

Here and there I spotted familiar faces from Bryanston Highschool, Damelin College, and a few from Wits University. Most of them had already cropped their hair short, in resigned preparation for their two-year stint away from *civi-street*. I stood and waited as the names were rattled off with military efficacy, watching, as one by one, the pallid faces hugged, kissed, and bade farewell to their innocence. Then, sooner than expected, the list of those designated for Kimberly was belted off in alphabetical order. Heart pounding like a bass drum, I listened, transfixed. Would anybody, on hearing my name shout out, "That's you, buddy, c'mon, get a move on?" Furtively, and just in case, I looked around for a familiar face in my proximity who might possibly recognize and betray me. At that very moment I heard my name uttered with objective clarity. For a moment it stood there, frozen in time, like some framed photograph. I imagined all the faces in the crowd turning my way: "*Eric Gerhard Müller*," pronounced in a thick South African accent – Müller pronounced, "MOOLAAH." No mistaking: my name, barked through the bullhorn with stark, terse authority. The moment passed, and the commanding voice continued his roll call, taking it for granted that a body would automatically step forth to report. It boggled my mind to think that I could now just walk up and give myself away – thus enter into a completely different life. Yet I knew that I'd be a traitor to myself if I did. Life demanded something different from me.

Not quite done, I followed the other recruits from my battalion down the hill to the waiting train that would take us to Kimberly. One of the uniformed officers looked at me with disdain, noting that I had no baggage, and said, "You can't be down here. You had your chance to say goodbye to your friends. Now get out of here. *If you say so*, I thought. Only now did I deign to turn my back on it all, while my mispronounced name resounded in my ears like a strange entity that had nothing in common with me – a sound sculpture, a gargoyle. That was the moment I was overcome with an acute sense of my own vulnerability. Sweat poured down my neck and face, and I increased my pace, and as soon as I'd crossed the pedestrian bridge I ran. Away, to be away from Milner Park, as fast and far as possible.

Only after I sat tucked away in a remote corner of the OK Bazaar's cafeteria did I feel autonomous enough to allow myself the luxury of relaxing. Though oily and weak, I slurped down the hot coffee and surrendered to a sense of ease. I ordered a second cup and a cheese sandwich. Intermittently, as I ate and sipped the cheap coffee, I fingered the one-way ticket to Switzerland. It was still reassuringly there, my ticket to freedom, new life. But I wasn't out yet. How long before they'd find out? How long before they'd come and search for me? How long before my name would appear on the A.W.O.L. list? Maybe they were already waiting for me back home?

They weren't, of course, but my paranoia plagued me for the rest of the afternoon. Every time I heard a door slam or the sound of a car outside my window, I froze, thinking that now surely, they'd

Part Two

come to get me. The afternoon crept by at a snail's pace and I was too tense to enjoy the final family teatime.

At last I stood at the threshold of departure: Jan Smuts Airport. After checking in, I bade my parents farewell and went through customs earlier than necessary. At the passport control, however, something in my stance or expression prompted the official to ask, "Have you completed your national service?"

The question took me off guard. I almost gave myself away, but squelched my fear and answered nonchalantly, "I don't need to, I'm a Swiss citizen," pointing to my Swiss passport. Of course, in my pocket I had my South African 'Identity Document.' He hesitated a moment, looked back at the passport, stamped it and waved me through. But I noticed that that he whispered something to a colleague, who then immediately slipped away. Would I be caught and apprehended, moments before takeoff?

I made it on board, found my seat, stowed away my luggage, sat down and buckled up. All the while I half expected an official to step on the plane and take me away. Not until we coasted along the runway, did the feeling of unease abate. Finally, the Boeing 747 lifted off, bumping through a few lightning infested storm clouds. At last I was spreading my wings. Free! I ordered a drink and sat back. I'd made it. I peered out the window at the blackness of the African Continent below; the city lights of Johannesburg were already left behind. For a moment I entertained the thought: *Where would I be now if I'd followed the voice of the megaphoned uniform?* – but quickly erased the answering images. Instead, I let my mind merge with the womb-like darkness, as my veins warmed through and widened with the soothing thrill of relief. I imagined hearing furtive drums beating across the vast expanse below me – a reassuring sonic vision. I lay back, huddled comfortably in my cot like seat, drawing the airline blanket over my legs. I didn't care about any tomorrows. The past turned over onto a blank new page. I didn't know, but it would take thirty-five years before I'd make it back to South Africa – a vastly different country, free of apartheid, though not of problems.

A Walk through Time and Snow

MY GRANDFATHER was a miller. To my left there's a framed photo of him and me standing inside the old wooden mill. He was also a carpenter and farmer, raising crops and keeping cows, sheep and goats. A black beret is pushed back over his high forehead, a pipe droops from the corner of his mouth, and he's wearing a faded brown, three-piece suit, not quite matching. His black and white polka dot tie is skew. He's leaning against the grinding mechanism with his elbow. I notice his hands look very much like mine do now. He has that confident and dignified look of a peasant who has worked hard his entire life, proven himself, braved many storms, and achieved respect, honor and standing in his community. I was five at the time the photo was taken – wearing a black turtleneck and looking serious, like my grandfather.

The mill, on the outskirts of Reckingen, is built next to a fast-flowing stream that runs into the Rhone, high up in the Swiss Alps, about ten miles from the *Rhoner Gletscher*. During the summer, as a kid, I loved watching the big paddle wheel go around and around. My great-grandfather built the mill. The flour and sawmill were handed down to my grandfather. The large, covered bridge crossing the Rhone in Reckingen is made from the timber that went through his mill. When the photo was taken, the mill was still in use. Now the mill is a museum, recognized as a cultural property of significance in the Canton of Valais. His name was Viktor, but I called him *Grossvater*.

When I was six we moved to South Africa. Because of the apartheid system I returned to Switzerland when I was twenty-one. Once I'd found a job in Basel, where I used to live as a child, I went to visit Grossvater, who was now well in his eighties. My aunt had moved into my grandfather's large farmhouse right next to the Rhone, and now cared for him. Apart from a few more wrinkles he looked unchanged. He still smoked his pipe or cigar, wore his black beret and a suit.

The morning after my arrival he asked whether I would join him for a walk up the valley to the next village. It was the middle of winter; the temperature was far below zero, and at least four feet of snow covered the ground. I was surprised that he wanted to undertake such a hike at his age and wondered how he'd fare, but I agreed immediately, glad to get out and do something. We dressed warmly and set out into the cold.

He didn't take the road as I thought he would, but chose a series of paths that crisscrossed along the foot of the mountains, used by cross-country skiers and farmers who brought their sheep down to the fountain in the center of the village. For a while the steep slope made going tough, and I was struck by his rapid pace. Furthermore, the usually taciturn man was talking while walking, pointing out landmarks all around, explaining their history and significance. He rarely turned around and I stuck close behind him to glean what he was saying, which remained fragmentary. Apart from the acoustical difficulties, he spoke *Wallisertiitsch*. For most Germans the Swiss dialect is difficult enough to understand, but the medieval sounding Alemannic dialect from the Canton of Valais is unintelligible even for some of the Swiss. But I loved the lilting, musical quality of the dialect that was both smooth like new snow and rugged like granite cliffs. I'd been exposed to it as a child, but I'd spent most of my life in South Africa, and was even struggling to recapture my *Baslerdütsch*. All along he held his extinguished pipe in his hand, pointing here and there with the stem. He was telling me the history, legends and myths of the surroundings. Every stream, cliff, mountain, gully, outcrop, ravine, waterfall, hillock, and chapel had a story. He told me of his own adventures as a boy and young man in these mountains where he'd lived his entire life; and of our ancestors, dating back to the 12th century. All the while he walked at a fast clip, while

I tried to keep up, panting behind him. Listening to him was like reading an exciting book with pages missing and others smudged.

Close to two hours later we descended into the village of Münster and settled into a *Gaststube*. He ordered *Glühwein* for us and lit his pipe. The mulled wine warmed me up immediately. Now that we were sitting, and there was nothing to point out, he lapsed back into silence and puffed on his pipe, watching the smoke rise. We relaxed, comfortable in the stretch of quiet. Not for long. Taking the last sip of warm wine, he said, "*Gömmer?*" stood up, and we left.

As we walked from the medieval village, a wizened old man opened a window above our heads and greeted him. Grossvater waved back, quipped something unintelligible, at which they both broke into loud laughter. As we marched on Grossvater dismissively called the man a little *bueb* who never left his house anymore, though only eighty. I smiled and we walked back home, this time along the level main road. Grossvater seemed oblivious of the traffic and walked in the middle of road, the way he'd done for decades. He wasn't going to change his ways and make room for the modern world. I was worried for his safety and what people would think. But nobody honked or got upset. Instead, they slowed down and carefully maneuvered around him, paying respects to the man from a different age, one of the last links between old and new – my grandfather, the miller.

Allen Ginsberg at the Atlantis

I USUALLY DON'T PUSH myself forward in a crowd, but this time I did. I cursed myself for not having arrived earlier. I'd suspected some interest in this iconic American Beat poet, but hadn't anticipated this kind of turn out, not here in Basel, Switzerland, at any rate. Slowly I wedged and weaseled my way forward on that chilly December evening in 1980, surprised at my own unscrupulous determination. The real shove, however, began when the green doors finally opened. I stood my ground aggressively to maintain my position, letting myself be thrust forward by the throng. When, at last, I'd made it to the entrance of the *Atlantis*, paid my seven Swiss francs, and stepped across the threshold, I straightway glanced around for a good place by the stage. Many small round tables, mooned by several low stools, were spaced in an erratic fashion all around the club, most of them taken. But there, up front to the right, next to the tower of PA boxes, I spotted a table and stool, provocatively vacant. *That's for me!* I jumped for it, my coat brushing into people's faces, as I frantically ran and hopped over stools to secure my place, claiming my territory not a second too soon. Nobody could block my view now, and I'd have a chance to observe Allen Ginsberg and his mates as much as I pleased, without feeling exposed myself. I could hardly believe my luck.

For the next hour I sat in alert abeyance, sipping beer, rolling and smoking Drum cigarettes, and scrutinizing my surroundings, reveling in the mounting anticipation. Up on the low stage, amidst the equipment of the resident rock group, stood three vacant chairs and a little table covered with a saffron cloth, on which Shivas danced. Neatly stacked, were his books and papers, as well as some small chimes, cymbals, sticks, and the famous portable harmonium (covered with stickers from his travels, including a backstage pass from Bob Dylan's *Rolling Thunder* tour) – relics themselves, conjuring up infamous episodes of the poet's life and work, triggering nostalgic images of the heyday of his influence: the flower-power demonstration through London, with Allen Ginsberg up front and everybody shouting, "We love you all, even the police"; the first momentous reading of *Howl*, so vividly described by Jack Kerouac; the hedonistic adventures shared with the other Beat poets; his openly homosexual escapades, paving the way for the gay liberation movement; his poems that capture the tenor of the sixties – fuming with rage, pity, awe, didactic cynicism… always agonizingly honest, forever trying to expose the Moloch of our age. And as I waited, I wondered to what extent Ginsberg and his work was still relevant, now, at the beginning of the eighties.

Nine p.m.! The radio guys recording the event gave the signal. They were ready. And there *he* was, right on time, appearing from the back, jovially making his way through the crowd, together with his two companions. I felt a slight pang of disappointment that he'd shaved off his down-to-his-belly beard. In true Ginsberg style – never predictable – he changed his mind, and with a hearty heady hoot, veered off to the left and headed for the loo. Some got up to follow him. Meanwhile, Ginsberg's companions nestled themselves comfortably in their seats, lighting incense and tuning their instruments – two guitars and a banjo. A waitress shoved a tray with a pot of tea, three glasses, and some sliced lemons under the table. At last, to chuckling applause, Ginsberg reappeared, stepping onto the platform with slow and deliberate steps, calmly taking his place in the center seat. His scraggy dark greying curls dropped round the back of his head and neck, his balding pate gleaming in the colored spotlights. He had the air of an eccentric professor, augmented by his trademark spectacles. Almost immediately the three of them broke forth in song and welcomed the crowd with a raunchy mantra – physical and earthy. The corners of his mouth lit up and the spectacles magnified the twinkle of his eyes. The vitality for which he was famous was still overabundantly alive. No getting into gear here. His feet pounded with the growing crescendo, both legs dancing, flapping, beating with happy-go-lucky synchronicity – up-down, up-down! The evening needed no further introduction, except for his two cohorts. The large, robust man, with waist-long, gently greying hair, turned out to be Peter Orlovsky, the farmer-poet who appears quite prominently in Jack Kerouac's autobiographical novels under different names. "Peter and I have lived in "heterosexual" harmony for the last twenty-seven years, and we both know each other very well indeed," declaimed the smiling Ginsberg, with Peter nodding enthusiastically, grinning provocatively. Peter wore an off-white baggy suit, which leant him a facade of formality. "And to my right," continued Ginsberg, we have Steven Taylor, a musician and poet… and we also know each other very well." Taylor, who had a shy innocence about him, would go on to tour with Allen for many years to come, and a few years later joined the countercultural band, The Fugs.

After the jocular intros, Ginsberg read some of his early poems, followed by excerpts from *Howl*. Songs peppered the repertoire, Ginsberg playing his little harmonium from India, the sticks or the hand-cymbals. Peter, all along, clapped, hollered, and screeched, his face a wonderwork of hilarious mimicry. In contrast, boyish Steven was quiet and subdued, delivering his songs in a tight, clean manner, every note in place. The first half closed with the iconoclast's most recent poems – all written within the last couple of years: short, concise, scathing, expositions of power, greed, injustices.

Peter pelted into the second half like a summer's storm into parched earth, rendering his orgiastic poetry with lightning power: sweat running down his face, hair flying and flailing about, his suit and shirt soaked and disheveled, coming undone to reveal a lusty paunch, pulsating along with the rhythm of his rhymes, the well-timed pauses framing ejaculatory outbursts of "*fuck, fuck, fuck.*" He whispered, sang and bellowed – my eardrums whacked soundly by the physical weight of his words as they plummeted forth from the speaker boxes next to which I sat. Orlovsky performed his guitar and

Banjo accompanied songs with percussive precision – this sweaty, blue-eyed, red-faced Bachus-farmer with the *"clean asshole."* And all the while a smiling Ginsberg applauding furiously, urging him to continue, "While he's hot!"

After a soothing and polished Taylor ear massage, it was back to Ginsberg, readings and songs, the most noteworthy being "Plutonian Ode," his 'epic' against atomic power, the arms race and the nuclear armament of the superpowers, which he read while standing, for emphasis and respect for the theme. This sonata of words began in largo, his sonorous and warm voice gradually moving into allegretto, lifting from that comfortable walking pace into a spirited allegro, followed by galloping *vivace*, and finally breaking forth into helter-skelter *vivacissimo* – a torrential downpour of words, a roaring crescendo of spitting, frothing and hissing; the fricatives, sonorants, and syllables splitting and cascading from his mouth; consonants crushed like pebbles in a maelstrom, vowels gasping for breath, words barely distinguishable as they catapulted through the audience with apocalyptic force. The doom-laden voice of conscience mesmerized the audience, kept us riveted and spellbound. After Ginsberg's climax and during the denouement, the pace diminuendoed and his voice relaxed for the downward glide. As he prepared for a soft landing, with the rapt audience hanging onto every syllabic utterance, someone shouted hysterically: "Stop it! Do you hear?" The words shot out like bullets in the night. Ginsberg continued to glide. Again, the frantic voice aimed and fired: "Do not go on! No more! I tell you, stop it at once!" Not the slightest response from Ginsberg. He kept reading as if he hadn't heard. The atmosphere in the capacity packed *Atlantis* was tense to the point of snapping. The frantic heckler, from the dark thickets of the galley above sniped on: "I told you to STOP! You don't know what you are saying!" Grandiosely, and with natural sovereignty Ginsberg paid not the slightest attention to the interloper, until he'd played his composition to the end – the last few words spoken *lento di molto*, which prolonged and stretched the tension to the utmost.... Only then did he sit down.

After a few moments of icy silence, Ginsberg asked, "Now sir,

Part Two

what are your objections?" He posed the question with severe composure.

Silence.

"Out with it... What do you find so objectionable?"

Silence.

Relentlessly, Allen Ginsberg stared into the audience's solar plexus from where the voice had issued, ready to pit himself against the most ferocious opposition.

Silence.

And Ginsberg waited, the wrath of God emanating from every pore; he transformed into a burning bush, though he sat serenely like Buddha under the Bodhi-tree. His beard appeared to grow on the spot, each second a year, and he became a rabbi, a patriarch – like the prophet Moses stepping down from Mount Sinai, having witnessed sacrilege. When the silence and his stature had expanded to the utmost, Ginsberg quietly said, "I will read the last part of the poem again, since some of you might have missed its significance, due to that **Hitlerian** interruption." And the word "Hitlerian" was uttered with deadly distinctiveness, which hovered in the air like a gaseous haze for many seeping seconds, until Ginsberg himself chose to dissolve it. He read without further interruption. The air was cleared.

The show was brought to an end with one of William Blake's poetic *Songs*. Again and again they repeated the innocent strain, "And all the hills echoed/And all the hills echoed/And all the hills echoed/And all the hills echoed..." with everybody joining in, Peter clapping and wailing his heart out, Steven strumming his guitar like a shepherd stroking his favorite lamb, and Ginsberg pumping his harmonium with gusto. On and on it went, nobody caring how long it would last. There was nothing sentimental about it, the mantric quality taking the audience back to the point of departure, only a rung higher.

Encores followed. We all partook of the tasty desserts – humorous poetic tidbits, little exhalations, post sixties flamboyance.

I would have loved to exchange a few words with that legendary poet, but hungry fans that stuck to him like burs immediately besieged him. And what would I have said to him anyway? I stepped into the cool night, satisfied and fulfilled. Ginsberg had not fallen prey to the vices of fame and fortune, in my opinion. He'd kept true to himself, had continued to be creative, standing up for his convictions – controversial and questionable as they would continue to be. Hurricane Ginsberg had – through his reading – swept and washed away the debris that had collected around me at the time. The reading had reconnected me to the power of the *word*, and inspired me to get back to writing.

The following morning as I walked by the *Sphinx* bookstore, I entered on a whim, went over to the English section and enquired whether they stocked any of Allen Ginsberg's work, only to be told that the poet himself was right upstairs signing books. Grabbing a copy of *The Fall of America* I bounded up the stairs, excited and tickled at the coincidence.

There he was, the great *Howl* himself, at ease, sitting behind a small desk in a little room, wearing jeans, and a garish yellow tie with blood red stripes (which nevertheless had a sunny air to it). Only two other people shared the space: a tall fashionable-dressed woman and a young man my age, who reminded me of Michael Jackson during the Afro phase. *What luck! No crowd.* The topic was meditation.

"How long are your daily meditations?" asked the sophisticated thirty-something woman in a lilting Swiss accent. She must have been almost seven feet tall, immaculately attired, skin remarkably smooth, her face enhanced through bold red lipstick, thick mascara.

"At least an hour a day," he answered. Turning toward me (away from the long-legged woman dressed in black), he asked with a quizzical smile, "Do you meditate, or have you ever had anything to do with meditation in the past?"

I blushed faintly, flattered and taken aback that Ginsberg had taken such immediate notice of me, though I felt exposed, put on the spot. A slew of thoughts raced through my mind – a type of self-confrontation. There was no escaping the moment. Allen patiently waited, looking at me through his thick spectacles. The simple question set into motion memory clots. I recalled my *astral traveling* attempts, my days trying to meditate under the Willow tree back in South Africa; mantras came to mind, learned from Fuzz, my Buddhist friend; and I remembered all those times I'd frantically attempted to empty my mind, to rid myself of *the Voice(s)* and those demons carried along by the putrid winds of my agonized mind, attacking me, crawling up my nose, into my ears and mouth, tasting like rot, to be spat out like pieces of soiled leather; or simply reverting to the archetypal *Om*. And then there were the many spiritually inclined books I'd read by writers like Carlos Castaneda, Lobsang Rampa, Sri Aurobindo, Helena Blavatsky, Krishnamurti, and more recently, Rudolf Steiner's *Knowledge of the Higher Worlds and its Attainments*, after reading Saul Bellows *Humboldt's Gift*. Too awkward to explain all this, I simply said, "Yes, I have."

"And who is or was your teacher?" Ginsberg continued to ask.

"I don't have one. I'm self-taught… well, kind of. I've read a number of books on the subject . . . and, of course, what friends have told me."

"You should get someone to teach you the basics."

"Maybe," I answered, adding with more confidence, "though I find myself critical of people who claim to be teachers after attending a couple of workshops, or those who call themselves Gurus, but go around milking people for money… and… well, you know."

Ginsberg laughed, "Oh, I understand perfectly well, but you must also know that it can be very dangerous to handle something like meditation by yourself. You need a guiding hand. Otherwise, your entry into otherworldly realms may be skewed, and your experiences warped. Faulty practices can work against you – to your detriment."

Before I could answer, the handsome young man with the Afro chirped up and said, "I always sing while meditating. I find it helps me concentrate," and he began singing, "Aum, aum, I am singing 'bout the word, that's the word, that's the word. Aum, aum, I'm a singing 'bout the word, that's the word, that's the universal word –" and he broke off, smiling, asking Ginsberg, "Do you also sing while meditating?"

Allen Ginsberg at the Atlantis

Ginsberg grinned and said, "I talk too much as it is. No, I prefer to meditate in silence."

The conversation amiably advanced onto different planes, unzipping diverse topics and themes – such as his experiences in Dakar, racism in South Africa and the world, reincarnation, consumerism, youth movements (professing he no longer had his finger on the pulse), and the Jack Kerouac School of Disembodied Poetics, which he founded.

In the course of the conversation, others entered the room, and not wanting to hog the Poet Laureate of the Counterculture, I made to leave, handing him the book to get autographed, which he did with a smile: *For Eric Axe* (my pseudonym for a while) - *Dharma, Love, Peace, Heart – Allen Ginsberg – Basel, December 3, 1980.*

"Look us up in Boulder, Colorado, if you ever come to America. You might want to study poetics at our school," and he wrote down the address on an index card for me. "Bye now," Ginsberg sang, and with that the man of 'angelic ravings' waved and blew me a farewell kiss.

I have always harbored a quiet pride at having received a personal invitation to Naropa University's Jack Kerouac School of Disembodied Poetics by the founder himself. Without a doubt, I recognized myself as a *disembodied* entity, which described my state at the time perfectly. It was comforting to know that others felt likewise. For the rest of the day I sat down by the Rhine, watching the turgid waters go by, reading through *The Fall of America*. And as I read the sometimes bleak but lucid, critical and rhapsodic poetic ramblings, I got a sense for the *other* America, the one imbued with the spirit of brother and sisterhood, the America aching to rise up from out of the toxic ashes of the old, to be built anew by those on the fringes, who will embody the *Dream* – the dreams of the tortured, oppressed and 'disembodied.' And I felt a yearning to be there, on the continent of endless possibilities – driven by the pursuit of *freedom*. A dream I fulfilled.

Stromboli

HUGO DIED the day he told me about Stromboli. I hardly knew him. He was a drummer and we'd played a few of gigs together after Tokolosh's acrimonious demise – the band I'd hoped would make me rich and famous.

Over a few beers in *Die Krone,* where local musicians often hung out, he told me about his recent trip to the volcano. His head bobbed in all directions as he spoke – punctuated by slugs of laughter – sending greasy strands of twisted, black hair across his Lennon glasses and pimpled cheeks, leaving only his long, scimitar nose free and glossy. I hadn't heard of this fire spewing isle off the southwest coast of Italy and its ongoing activity over the last 2000 years. And I thought it a gross exaggeration when he claimed that it still erupts about every fifteen minutes. I was amused by his effusiveness and vivid descriptions of the eruptions, reinforced by fun facts such as Jules Verne depicting Axel and Otto Lidenbrock emerging from that volcano at the end of his novel, *Journey to the Center to the Earth.* Nevertheless, my interest was piqued. "You should go," Hugo said, as he left, slapping me on the shoulder.

He hitched a ride home, but didn't bother to buckle up, as he only lived a few miles out of Schwenningen, in the heart of Germany's Black Forest. At a hairpin turn, halfway down a hill the blue VW bug rolled over and crashed into a ditch. Hugo died immediately. The driver escaped without a scratch.

I was between jobs, and instead of attending Hugo's funeral I packed my backpack, jumped on a train and headed south. I'd pay my respects differently. Besides, now that Tokolosh had broken up, there was really no reason for me to remain in Germany. I'd worry about the future on my return. For the moment it was just good to get out.

After a stop in Milan to view Leonardo da Vinci's *Last Supper* and changing trains in Naples, I finally made it on the night train to Sicily. However, after crossing the Straits of Messina, with the entire train shunted onto the ferry, I took the wrong connection and traveled down Sicily's rocky east coast past Mt. Etna, almost all the way to Catania before I realized my mistake. Getting off at a forlorn station I waited an hour before I managed to catch a packed train back to Messina and finally to Milazzo. I'd missed the ferry and had to spend a night in a cheap hotel, kept awake by pounding disco music from across the road.

The almost six-hour ferry crossing was relaxing and pleasant, except for a short interlude where I almost got into a tangle with some jealous Italians. I was sitting peacefully at a large table drinking coffee, reading up on Stromboli from a guide book, when a gaggle of pretty Italian schoolgirls descended around me. They immediately showered me with questions, delighted to try out their English skills, and insisting I share in their delicious sandwiches. I succumbed to their ebullient charm, not noticing a posse of guys approaching who thought I was flirting with their girls. The head honcho rudely and roughly slapped me on the shoulder and hurled insults at me in Italian, arms gesticulating. Immediately the girls came to my defense, which only upset him more. At last he said, "What-sa your name, huh?" I told him, adding that I came from South Africa, ignoring the fact that I now lived in Germany and was also Swiss. At the mention of Africa, he broke into a wide smile. At once he sat down next to me and explained that his uncle had moved to Africa. Inexplicably, I was now his buddy and he bought me another cup of coffee. The other three guys happily squeezed in next to the girls, and after a while I bade the happy bunch farewell. For the rest of the ferry crossing, whenever he saw me, he waved and shouted, "Africa, amico mio."

In the distance the conical mountain, with a tassel of white smoke on top, rose steadily from the calm blue Mediterranean. I hurried to the ferry's bow and watched it grow, rapt. Arriving at the port of Stromboli I first made my way to the black sand beach in search of a place to sleep. The ferry was only slated to return in two days; a forced disconnect from the rest of the world – a fact I relished. And I found a perfect spot between two lava stumps that offered a modicum of shade – rare on this sparsely treed island. Hiding my backpack in the low, but dense vegetation behind the rocks, I sauntered off to the village of Stromboli to get a bite to eat. After a tasty plate of spaghetti al pomodoro, washed down by cool beer, I strolled back to my rocky abode to get a good night's sleep. As I came to my lowly shelter I found – to my annoyance – someone else's rucksack and rolled out sleeping bag. So much for that, I thought, and went to retrieve my backpack.

"Hullo, I just went to take a shit." I spun around and came face to face with a small, stocky young man, wearing nothing but his tightywhities. "I'm Quentin." He stretched out his hand. "Looking for a place to sleep, are yer?" I nodded, trying to place his British accent, shaking his hand with some hesitancy, hoping he was a lefty.

"Eric's the name... yeah, and I'd hoped to sleep right here."

"Be my guest, there's room for two. Good to meet you, mate." He scratched his head vigorously with both hands, digging his fingers into his short, thick red hair. "So, I presume you're going to scale the volcano, yeah? Good, we can climb together... come on, make yourself comfortable." For the rest of the evening Quentin, a jovial London taxi driver, kept me entertained with farfetched stories of hilarious and harrowing exploits around London Town.

The next morning we took a quick dip in the ocean, after which Quentin insisted on shaving, nicking his freckled cheeks and neck in the process. Refreshed, we set out and found a café, canopied with bougainvillea, where we enjoyed a cappuccino and Panini sandwich. We didn't linger too long as it was warming up fast. Asking for directions we found the trail leading up the volcano behind the San Vincenzo church. The path was well worn and snaked through dense macchia, which gave off a fragrant smell that grew in pungency with the heat and sound of cicadas. Soon the series of switchbacks increased and the vegetation gave way to barren steep slopes. We hadn't brought any water with us and felt a touch thirsty. Both of us wore sandals with little traction, and the solid path became sandy and coarse, causing us to slide back with almost every step we took. But the view was spectacular and we gradually made our way up this massive volcanic cone. A few robust hikers, stocked and well equipped with boots, drink and victuals passed us. As we neared the summit the rising plume became more visible and we could hear the intermittent rumble of the eruptions.

Three hours later and way past noon we finally reached Pizzo Sopra La Fossa, the summit, 924 meters above sea level. The clear sky and blue water almost merged seamlessly at the horizon, and from where we stood, we had a 360-degree view of the expansive Tyrrhenian Sea. In the distance we spied the other six volcanic Aeolian Islands of the archipelago. But most riveting of all were the craters with their various vents about 100 to 150 meters below us. Paths crisscrossed and led down to them from our ideal viewing terrace. It was surprisingly chilly, but the large, rounded lava ledge, which was the rim of the original crater, was like a colossal oven, warmed through by the molten mass deep down under. Only a thin funnel of smoke issued and merged from the vents, and stillness pervaded the air, which made me wonder whether the volcano did erupt every fifteen minutes. Soon enough I heard the heralding rumble – sounding much louder, now that we were in full view of the crater. Within seconds, and accompanied by a loud boom, basaltic magma jetted hundreds of feet into the air. Quentin screamed in exaltation, dancing a jig on his stocky legs. "They usually come in threes, or so——." Before he could finish the sentence, another thunderous explosion, far louder, cut him off. A rush of adrenalin pumped through my system, and I thought of Hugo. The third eruption, though muted, released a thick plume of ash that spread like a dark, menacing cumulus cloud, before dissipating.

Throughout the rest of the afternoon we watched ash and lava blocks spout from the colossal blowhole of this black leviathan. Mostly we had the volcano to ourselves, and those who came only stayed for a few eruptions. One American reached the summit just as it blasted its first batch of slugs into the air after a twenty-minute respite. "Is that all," he said dismissively. "Not very impressive." I knew better, but kept mum. Seconds later the loudest explosion so far hurled ejecta and ash rocketing sky high – Stromboli was clearly giving the American the molten finger. "How awesome is that!" and he immediately lifted his video camera to his face and filmed the spectacle. "Got it," he quipped, and without a second glance turned around and jogged back down. He'd stayed for five minutes, tops.

Quentin had gone off to find a comfortable place to snooze, leaving me alone with my thoughts. I considered the island's mythic origin, picturing the disgruntled master craftsman Hephaestus, Greek God of fire and volcanoes, hurling the island Thira into the Tyrrhenian Sea, resulting in the birth of Stromboli. And I wondered whether Stromboli was the floating Aeolian island visited by Odysseus, home to King Aeolus – master of winds, who'd given the Achaean the sack of wind, which would have ensured his safe return to Ithaca, had he not fallen asleep. From my vantage point the island certainly seemed to be swimming free in the cobalt blue expanse. Like Odysseus I was trying to find my own Ithaca, and though I didn't know it yet, contrary winds would blow me off course for a number of years to come – it's hard to remain awake and not be betrayed by the mutinous crew of one's own shortcomings. But I also thought of Hugo, our chance meeting, why he had to die so young, his spiritual whereabouts, and the afterlife. Was I given another chance? At what?

An hour later I descended toward the crater, following one of the many paths to the edge, feeling some trepidation as I recalled more stories from the guide book – of people getting injured, even killed by falling lava bombs (one reason why guides became compulsory a few years after my visit). I was barefoot and it was like stepping across the back of some gigantic, lumbering, prehistoric sauropod, approaching its gaping, fire-spewing jaw and nostrils. As the earth growled from the depths of its volcanic bowels, signaling another burst of gas about to shoot hundreds of tons of matter all around, I felt the earth tremble beneath my feet. When the eruption occurred,

I could hear and feel the blocks as they hit the ground near to me. I took the hint and walked back to the safety of the upper terrace.

Subtleties can take one by surprise. Up to now the magnitude and sonic volume of the eruptions had impressed me the most, but I hadn't bargained for the array and nuances of color I now witnessed as the afternoon wore on and the sun lowered toward the horizon. What had appeared as grey-white ash and black ejecta now took on color. The most gentle and veiled pink began to appear midst the ash emissions. The lucid rose red gradually gave way to orange and shades of cherry red, until it turned to a rich crimson and ruby. I wanted to hug Hugo for telling me about the wonders of Stromboli. It exceeded by far the best lightshow and fireworks I'd seen. I felt close to the gods. Each eruption became a prayer, and Gaia's primal display and guttural ululations became Hugo's memorial service. I felt his spirit near – I saw and heard his laughter, punctuated by terrific explosions. I was paying my respects – each incandescent fountain of lava was a funeral rite. I had a vision of Hugo giving his last drum solo, perched on top of the volcano, beating to the rhythms of the eruptions. My head felt like a 'spinning top,' at one with the meaning of Stromboli's original name – *Strongyle*.

Now that it was dark, more people had arrived to witness the fountains of molten rock exploding, often simultaneously from different vents. Intermittently, lava flows ran down the far side of the mountain, known as the Sciara del Fuoco. Quentin, who'd wandered off near the crater's edge sat down next to me. I had almost forgotten about him. He smiled and said softly, "Good stuff." I nodded. "Want some," and he offered me a bottle of water." Seeing the water, I suddenly realized how thirsty I was.

"Gee, man, where did you get that from?" I shouted, almost grabbing the bottle from him.

"A girl I met," and he pointed over to a group of young people to our left. I'll be seeing her later," and he nudged me with his elbow and winked.

"You scoundrel, you," I said, shaking my head, laughing. We sat in silence for a few more eruptions before we got up and descended.

Part Two

In the light of the moon that rose in the west we ran stretches of the trail, pausing only to catch our breath. We made it down in just over an hour. Quentin accompanied me back to the beach, got his haversack, and with a "See you, mate," disappeared into another tale in the making. I never did see him again.

I had the entire beach to myself and I stretched out comfortably in my sleeping bag, peering up at the stars and listening to the ocean's gentle sibilance. The last time I saw so many stars so clearly was in the African Highveld. And it was strangely reassuring to know that almost a thousand meters above me the volcano was still popping like a champagne bottle, mirroring microcosmically the universe with its fountains of incandescent sparks. I felt as safe, alive and fulfilled as I hadn't in a long while. "Hugo, my buddy, thanks for showing me this *Lighthouse of the Mediterranean*– may your soul soar in peace."

7 Trains, 7 Planes:
A Blessing

DUE TO my mother's ongoing debilitating and deteriorating illness, my parents had missed the birth of both our sons and our wedding. Though only in her mid-fifties, her traveling days – which she'd loved so much – were conclusively over. At least we'd once made it over to Eugene, Oregon, so they could meet Tina. Even without Tina's pregnancy, it had been an ordeal: delayed flights, missed busses, trouble at the border (because of some homeopathic 'drugs' we'd brought along for my mother), and a skanky motel. Since then we talked regularly over the phone once a week. I was surprised when she called again, only a couple of days after our last call.

"How are you?" I asked.

Pause. "Um… not well." That's when I knew my mother would die. Over the years I'd come to expect her perfunctory *I'm fine* reply. In a whisper she added: "It's time." I pressed the handset to my ear and waited. Usually, she'd tell me about this or that, who'd come by, what they'd said or done; the weather. Save for the heightened pulse ringing through my ears, amplified by the receiver – nothing.

"Not doing well?" I asked, unable to dispense with the habitual oblique talk.

"No." Part of me still expected to hear the usual *but, don't worry, all will be fine.*

"Should I come?"

"Yes…."

"I'll make arrangements."

"Thank you. Here's your father."

Part Two

That was the last time I spoke to her on the phone. Dad confirmed my fears "It's best you come now."

In our family nucleus we struggled to express feelings openly, though the love was unconditional. We settled on euphemisms or dispensed with them entirely. For instance, when my brother and I talked on the phone we'd say, "Have you talked to the *West Coast* recently?" or "How's *Eugene*?"

To get to Eugene, Oregon, was easier said than done. At the time we lived in Bochum-Langendreer, Germany, separated by five and a half thousand miles. Tina had just given birth to our second son and I had teaching and piano accompanying obligations. Furthermore, I was about to perform with a dance troupe for which I'd composed a lengthy piece of music. We were in the midst of rehearsals, and nobody else could play the piano part, since my notation consisted of illegible signs and squiggles that only I could decode. Besides, we had no money for the flight. With my low paying jobs as an accompanist and substitute teacher we barely got by.

Necessity puts things in motion. Our neighbors fronted us the money. I got time off school and the director of the troupe reluctantly accepted my leave of absence, as long as I promised to be back in time for the show. Early next morning, while Tina organized the plane tickets, I drove to the American consulate in Bonn to secure my visa, which was still required back in the mid-eighties. When I saw the long lines, I despaired. At this rate I'd never make the evening flight. However, as soon as I explained my reason for visiting the US, they offered their condolences and gave me preferential treatment. I was out within twenty minutes, the required documents in hand. That same afternoon Tina drove me to the local train station in Langendreer, where I boarded the first of seven trains. The long trip had begun.

I changed trains in Bochum and arrived in Düsseldorf just in time to catch the plane to Amsterdam, where I spent a rough and sleepless night stretched out on a hard airport bench, before flying off to Heathrow. An unexpected flight delay made me anxious, but we finally got clearance to board. With my standby ticket in hand I watched and waited as the other passengers filed past the gate agent and walked down the jet bridge. At such short notice and with limited budget, Tina hadn't been able to procure assigned seating for the long flights. It made getting a seat a gamble, but I managed to get a window seat in the last row. *Would Mom hang on till Georg and I arrived?*

I passed through security at JFK International Airport in New York without a hitch. Luckily, I didn't I have a lengthy layover, though I again waited nervously for the scheduled passengers to board. A friendly agent noticed my mounting unease and assured me there'd be enough seats available.

I arrived in Seattle jetlagged and exhausted. Catching a bus into the city, I checked into a cheap motel within walking distance of the train station. Early next morning, I looked for a bank to cash one of my traveler's check. Except for some homeless people huddled on a sidewalk, sharing joints and swigging from a brown paper bag, the streets remained deserted. It being Sunday, no banks were open. Fortunately, an affable receptionist at a posh hotel took pity on me and cashed one of my checks. I celebrated with a coffee and bagel down at the station. An hour later I sat on the train, impressed by the untamed and expansive beauty of the Pacific Northwest, and humored by a tangle-bearded white-haired conductor who looked like he had just stepped off a Western movie set. He claimed to have served on this "Old Chief's Train," as he called it, for over two decades. At about five in the afternoon I finally trundled into the Eugene station, met by my father, visibly aged.

"She's determined to hold on," Dad said as we drove up to the house, "until you and Georg arrive."

"When's he coming?"

"In four days. He can't come any earlier… obligations." Georg lived in Dornach, Switzerland at the time.

"Ah… I'm leaving that same morning. Pity. Got a show to play, you know." Dad didn't respond. "So, I guess I won't see him." This meant we'd miss out on the last opportunity to be united as a family. The four of us hadn't been together for years – not since Georg and I left South Africa. And that was seven years ago.

Part Two

"Brace yourself," he said after a while. She's..." He cleared his throat, leaving the sentence hovering.

I looked around the living room as we entered through the garage door, greeted by familiar smells, though layered with a faint odor of decay. Different house, same decorations. As a family we'd moved many times, but the paintings, African statuettes, books, the old Grotrian Steinweg piano, crystal glassware, hand painted antique Chinese porcelain, and sundry disparate knickknacks, remained comfortingly the same. They transported me back to my childhood for a few fleeting moments. I hesitated, lingering in the past, delaying the moment of walking down the short, carpeted passage to where my mother lay.

As I stepped into the darkened bedroom, two stick arms raised themselves from the muddle of sheets and blankets. The physical shock of her emaciated body left me trembling. Holocaust pictures flashed up against my will. To hide my emotions, I immediately bent over to greet her, surprised at the strength of her embrace. She mumbled a few inaudible words, let go, and looked up at me, her eyes as alive and sparkling as ever. Then she raised her spindly arms once more and hugged me all over again. When she finally let go, she tapped the side of the bed and whispered, "Sit." I sat and took hold of her hand, surprised at the current of energy that shot through her fingers into mine, her vibrant hand at such odds with the withered and shrunken body. I thought of all the piano she'd played throughout her life, from the days as a child prodigy in Durban, South Africa – performing and playing concertos years before she'd reached her teens – all the way through to a few weeks ago when she was finally and unequivocally moored to her bed. The cumulative focus that had gone into her fingers over the decades still emanated. Her arms and body were cold, but her hands were warm – alive.

"I'm sorry, I can't talk very well... look," and she opened her mouth to reveal swollen tongue and gums, patched with white inexplicable growths. She shut her mouth and smiled. "I'm glad you came," and she squeezed my hand. "Don't think of me as dying..." She coughed and her face went taught. "Water," and she pointed to

7 Trains, 7 Planes: A Blessing

a crystal bowl on the bedside table. I put the glass to her lips. She struggled to drink just a few sips. "Better, thanks…" She looked at me resolutely. "Just think of this as a visit… like any other… not the end. The real me will always live on and be with you." She smiled, and I saw the little girl in her, and the mother I knew when I was a little boy.

Her baffling condition had started almost imperceptibly, when she was still in her early forties: dizzy spells, light headedness, growing fatigue. Initially, she thought nothing of it, persevering energetically with her manifold activities, which included performing, singing and music lessons, composing, accompanying, studying for her B.Mus degree (which was followed by a Master's degree in music), and keeping the household afloat. Through it all she never complained, kept her composure, and bore it all with a smile, but the fainting spells continued and became more acute and frequent. We became silent witnesses to her relentless and gradual decline. Simply going for a walk or a short outing became an ordeal. She'd have to bend over or sit down every few minutes to fight off the fainting spells. Moreover, she was Oma's main caregiver, caring for our beloved grandmother to the bitter end.

Mom's mystery sickness worsened incrementally and no doctors could heal, let alone diagnose her successfully. Yet, she persisted, going from one physician to the next, from hospital to hospital, with a never-ending battery of tests that never offered any conclusive results. The medications she received only exacerbated her affliction. When allopathic medicine failed her, she tried acupuncture, herbalists, faith healers and quacks of every ilk. Not one of them made a positive difference, and her body continued to deteriorate – a steady decline spanning a decade and a half.

During the next three days I played piano for her, taking over the household chores to relieve my father, and hosting the visitors who dropped by, making sure they didn't stay too long. I was moved to witness how well loved my mother was in this new community, in which they'd only lived for the past five years. Mid-morning and afternoons I made tea for two, though she couldn't drink a drop.

I anyway set the tray with her favorite Royal Doulton Norfolk Vintage Bone China teacup, and prepared the tea the way she loved and was used to. It made sitting by her bedside homey and intimate. These were my favorite moments – just the two of us. She'd close her eyes, breathe deeply, and whisper, "Ah, Earl Grey." We talked, laughed, and reminisced, returning randomly to all the places we'd lived in South Africa, Germany, and Switzerland. She tired easily, and sometimes we just sat in silence. I showed photos of Edmund and Matthew, her two grandchildren she'd never met. She held and stared at the photos for a long time, eyes moist. Mostly, she fell asleep while I talked to her.

In the evenings my father and I sat together, long into the night. We did not talk about her impending death; instead he reminisced about growing up in the Swiss Alps, leaving the Catholic Church, apprenticing as a Swiss watchmaker, moving to South Africa, meeting Mom, and his circuitous spiritual path. In between I tried to steer the conversation back to the present, but he deflected, recalling how he was diagnosed with tuberculosis, which almost killed him, and his decision to become a Waldorf teacher at the age of forty – stories I'd often heard before. In relating his own stories, he was also traversing his life with Christa, his wife.

The three days rolled into one and passed all too quickly. The morning of my departure she called me in right after I'd done the breakfast dishes. "Come close." I sat down. "Closer… I want to bless you. You don't have to feel embarrassed." Her voice trailed away in a throaty whisper. I bent down low and she kissed me on the forehead and put her hands against my cheeks. She added a few unintelligible words. I remained quiet, not wanting to break the mood. Her green tourmaline eyes were extraordinarily clear. "Now, say goodbye, turn around and go. We don't need to make this sentimental. You know I love you." I gave her one last hug, then did as I was told.

"I love you too… goodbye." I turned and left.

As I sat on the train to Portland, I became increasingly aware of an inexplicable shift within me. I wondered why I was feeling so good – euphoric – given that I had just left my dying mother and that I would never see her again. A calm ecstasy settled over me as I peered out the train window. No pain, no grief, no sorrow, just warm and light filled, within and around me. I realized it had begun the moment she'd kissed me on the forehead, but I hadn't quite registered the gravitas of the moment. For the first time in my life I understood and recognize the power of *blessing* – a true, authentic, selfless blessing. A gift from the core of her being. Love. Her blessing has remained one of the most profound experiences in my life, both tangible and otherworldly.

In Portland I endured another dose of the *standby blues,* and the agent at the gate warned me that I probably wouldn't get a seat since the flight was booked to capacity. I didn't care and I made it on board after all. I found my seat, gave thanks to the *no-show* passenger, and snoozed all the way to New York, from where I hopped across the pond to Heathrow with no trouble. But things never go smoothly for too long and I tolerated hours of tedious delay before I caught my seventh and last flight to Amsterdam.

I would love to have gone to the van Gogh or Rijksmuseum, but I made do with dawdling through the picturesque streets of Amsterdam and enjoying a cup of coffee and some *stroopwafels* next to a canal before locating and boarding the train. I sat alone in my compartment when a bearded and disheveled man joined me. Seconds after seating he broke into tears, explaining that he'd been robbed and desperately needed some money to get to Germany. He could barely get his breath and his hands were shaking as he pushed his ruffled long hair from his puffy eyes. He promised to pay me back. Feeling sorry for him, I pulled out some banknotes and handed them to him. Immediately he stopped crying, and ran out. I chased after him, but he leaped from the train, flipped me off, and disappeared into the crowd. I'd fallen victim to my own gullibility. After my anger had subsided, I laughed at the incident.

The train departed, and with the steady rhythm of the rails my thoughts returned to my mother and the last three days I'd spent with her. My numbed mind gave way to a tableau of images from our shared life, reaching back to my childhood, capturing the myriad acts of kindness, moments of unconditional love. I let the vignettes pass by as my eyes stared vacantly out the window. After changing trains in Duisburg, I was overcome with fatigue and a melancholia that bordered on depression, gnawing at my bones. I wanted to cry, but the tears dammed up in my throat. Finally, I made it onto the seventh and last train from Bochum to Langendreer, from where I still had to catch a bus to our *Siedlung*, our residential area. No sooner had I climbed up the three flights of stairs to our apartment when the phone rang: She'd died.

To this day I regret not having cancelled the show that could have gone on without me, one way or another. But for a misguided sense of duty I'd sacrificed our final family reunion – an opportunity forever lost – for a performance. The following evening, as I sat down at the piano, my mother's spirit descended and touched me. The curtain opened, I let her in, and through me she did what she loved most – play piano.

"Water, Water"

BACK IN THE FALL of 1990, I marched my sixteen fourth graders down the hill to the Convalescent Center in Eugene, Oregon, armed with recorders, three music stands and pages of sheet music. Free of the classroom, the girls began to skip and hop happily along the road, while some of the boys punched and chased each other. "Not too wild," I admonished, "and watch out for cars."

At the front gate I gathered my flock and reminded them to be on their best behavior. "Listen up! The seniors in this eldercare facility don't get visitors very often, or live entertainment from young people like you. It's a real treat for them and they are looking forward to our arrival. We're here to put some light, life and music into their hearts. Let's go and give them our best."

The nursing staff welcomed us warmly and led us into a large common room where several seniors were already waiting for us, most of them in wheelchairs. As we set up the music stands and unpacked our recorders, more arrived, using walkers, quad canes, or were rolled in by nurses. The students got very quiet in the presence of these old people who'd reached the end of their lives while they were just starting out. Some of the elderly were attached to ventilators, while others looked vacant, adrift in various stages of dementia.

After a short and hearty introduction on my part we launched into our medley of songs, interspersed with three- and four-part recorder pieces. I was proud of my students who surpassed themselves. They sang like angels, behaved impeccably, and played their recorders better than in the classroom. A few of the elderly sang along as soon as they recognized a familiar round, spiritual or folk song. A number of them had tears in their eyes, and I had to think of my own grandmother who'd spent her last few months in a nursing home – how she'd cherished our visits. The memory pushed a lump into my throat and I felt guilty for not having visited her more often.

Toward the end of our recital, a spindly woman on a raised hospital bed, hooked to an IV drip and nasal tubes, started to moan unintelligibly. The young African American male nurse at her side tried to calm her down, but she continued groaning in her feeble voice, which steadily grew more persistent and louder. She repeated the same word again and again. The nurse smiled, gestured for us to continue and wheeled her out. The words "Water, water," were now clearly audible, fading down the hallway behind the glass doors.

Once we'd packed up and were about to take our leave, the friendly male nurse reappeared. "Sorry about the interruption. Your music moved her. I could tell. She's our oldest senior here – next year she'll turn a hundred. You heard her mumble, "Water, water"; well, that's because she's one of the last people to have crossed America on the Oregon Trail in a covered wagon. She was just a little girl at the time, three or four years old. They ran out of water and the family nearly died. That experience marked her for life. However, the trek was also the happiest of her life. But now, the only words she ever utters, is 'Water, water.'"

We returned to our classroom deeply touched, having experienced a living link to American history.

We Met at The Met

WET SUNDAY MORNING. I began selling my books in a makeshift booth, shielding them from bolshie wind-gusts and vagrant rain pellets. Futile. People scurried by, heads down, on this cold, rainy day at the Fall Farm Fair in upstate New York! Business was bound to be scanty. I didn't care; even the sale of one book is *whoopee* worthy.

Before long, my lips turned blue, which they remained for the rest of the day, though I combated the coloration and cold with cups of hot coffee. Intermittently, the rains eased and I enjoyed a few routine and friendly conversations with passersby, though my book piles remained undiminished. Around noon the sun peeked through and I talked a browser into buying my children's book, *The Invisible Boat*, for his 9-year-old son, who fondled the book, staring longingly at the evocative cover – three kids, a dwarf and a water sprite on a small boat, sailing through rough waters in which a one-eyed monster lurks. The rains returned and people sought shelter – elsewhere.

After the downpour a woman with her young daughter stopped, dawdled, and carefully fingered through my entire selection in silence, all eight books, not looking up once. Eventually, she picked up *Meet Me at the Met* for the third time, met my eye and said that her father had worked as a docent at the Metropolitan Museum of Art for many years. Duly impressed and glad to find someone who had a connection to that cultural epicenter, I declared, a bit too effusively, that it was my favorite museum in the world, even over and above the Louvre and Uffizi, after which I delivered my perfunctory two-sentence plot summary of the novel. She nodded, smiled and said, "I'll take it." To my delight she also bought the children's book for her daughter. By 4 p.m. and one more sale I called it quits, went home, and warmed myself up by the woodstove.

About ten days later I received an unexpected email:

Dear Eric,

My daughter, Marina, obtained this book from you, inscribed to me (Peter). I find your book very interesting, in particular since I have served as a Docent at The Met since 2005. I am familiar with all the images in your book.

Sincerely,
Peter Kubicek

P.S. If you are willing to give me your precise home address, I would like to reciprocate by mailing you MY book

I was thrilled. It's always a great pleasure to receive some echo about one's writing. Any interest is honored. And his intention to send me a copy of his book was a welcome bonus. Curious as to what kind of book he'd written I immediately googled him, assuming it was about art. Instead, I was surprised to discover that his book, *Memories of Evil: Recalling a World War II Childhood*, dealt with his experiences in *six* different German concentration camps. He was holocaust survivor!

From then on, I received emails from Peter every few days, some personal, others to a select group of friends and acquaintances. He attached links to articles or YouTube videos about the Holocaust, anti-Semitism, or current political issues – mostly his concern about the rise of Trump.

When *Memories of Evil* arrived, I read the slim volume in two intense sittings, after which – compelled to convey my thoughts – I shot him an email. His prompt, understated reply ended with, "Now that I have finished reading your interesting book [...] I think it's time that we met – obviously at The Met." I was delighted, and we agreed to meet on Thursday, December 22nd at 11 a.m.

My wife and I departed early to allow for some coffee before the scheduled meeting. Peter had made it clear that he first wanted to make the rounds of the museum before inviting us to the Staff Dining Room. But I need my coffee before I embark on any artistic tour – and besides, it's a long-standing tradition Martina and I have shared for years. That morning the traffic was surprisingly fluid, and we made it down in just over two hours, arriving precisely at 10 a.m. – opening time. We were the first customers at the American Wing Café, and the Cappuccino was surprisingly good (the quality vacillates). How luxurious to sit once again in that spacious airy atrium, surrounded by all those sculptures, with the morning light shining through the expansive skylights. We hadn't frequented the Met for at least eight months. High time.

Close to 11 a.m., via the Equestrian Court, we strolled to the designated meeting place: the lower coatroom situated by the 81st street entrance. He said he'd wait for us by the wood benches at the end of the narrow gallery. He'd sent me a photo of him standing in front of Jackson Pollock's *Autumn Rhythm*, (Number 30) so that I would recognize him. We were a couple of minutes early and Martina disappeared into the adjacent gift shop. A minute later an elderly man with white hair and chin-curtain beard rounded the corner, wearing an official Met nametag, bearing the headshot of the photo he'd sent me. "Peter?" I asked, approaching him. I think he expected me to look different, because he hesitated before shaking my outstretched hand. He appeared older, smaller and more delicate than I had imagined, based on the photo – almost elfin. Martina joined us at that moment, and I introduced them, after which she departed, promising to meet up with us in the Great Hall at 12:30 by the octagonal information desk.

After Martina left, he said, looking straight at me, "I only have two questions about your book. First, is it fictional or true?"

"Mostly fictional, though some biographical details are woven into the novel."

"Second: why do you spell your name, Müller, with an umlaut?" I was taken aback, but I explained that I was being true to my Swiss heritage, and that two of our mills up in the Swiss Alps, built by my grandfather and great grandfather, are still intact, though they've now been turned into museums. He looked at me quizzically, and then, without another word, turned to start the tour. I followed him up the stairs, wondering whether he deemed it bad that my name has an umlaut. It does accentuate the German element. I shrugged it off.

We slowly made our way through the Greek and Roman galleries, passing through the Great Hall to the Byzantine exhibit underneath the Grand Stairway, and onward to the medieval gallery in which the Christmas tree and Neapolitan Crèche was installed. He stopped and gestured toward the exquisitely decorated spruce, reaching over 20 feet above us, adorned with a host of finely crafted angels and cherubs – an annual installation going back to the 1960's. He fixed his gaze at the multifaceted nativity scene, murmured something inaudible, and moved on.

As we walked along he commented on various art pieces, and told little anecdotes of his time as a docent, from which he'd resigned a couple of years ago, though he still enjoyed the docent emeritus status, which came with perks, such as free entrance, access to some restricted areas, and selected discounts. Most of the general information was familiar to me, having researched the Met quite exhaustively while writing *Meet Me at the Met*. However, he stopped in front of many artworks that I had usually bypassed, which was refreshing, besides giving me insights into the man who had gone through so much trauma, seen the worst of humanity, and experienced manifestations of evil, first hand. I was touched by the love he exhibited toward these masterpieces, and surprised by some of the artwork he pointed out, like a small finely crafted wooden relief of Christ being lifted from the cross, or the European tapestries from the Late Middle Ages and Early Renaissance. His deep appreciation for artistic skill and delicacy shone through. Usually I connect to individual pieces based on my own insights and inclinations, but now I was looking at the art through his eyes, his world.

We continued our leisurely, perambulation though the European Petrie Sculpture Court, viewing *Perseus* and Rodin's *The Burghers of Calais,* which he loved. I was only half attentive to his words, thinking of him as a child, separated first from his father, who had luckily made it out of Czechoslovakia in time, and later from his mother and the rest of the family, when they were sent to Bergen-Belsen, where his mother remained, while he was shuttled through five more camps. What must that do to a person, especially during the vulnerable formative years? As we walked from gallery to gallery, I tried to find out more about him, but he eluded my queries by pointing to a painting, or simply refraining from answering. Occasionally he offered some insights into his family, an anecdotal reference to his wife, twin daughters, or his grandchildren.

Up at the modern art galleries we met up with Martina by chance in the Lila Acheson Wallace Wing. It was just past noon, and from then on, she stayed with us. Via the Impressionists and Expressionists, we meandered toward the Asian art section, which was his favorite. Another surprise. On the way we stopped off at the Drawings and Prints offices, where we met Allison Rudnick, the assistant Curator, and another woman who was copying one of Rubin's exquisite drawings. Alison had been on a tour to India with Peter and his wife, and within seconds she got him to laugh as they reminisced. It was heartening to observe Peter, who'd appeared somewhat dour and withdrawn, relax and lighten in her convivial company. Allison invited us to make an appointment to view the hundreds of prints and drawings whenever we wanted to. We are still determined to take her up on the offer.

By now my legs were aching. It was getting close to one o'clock. Martina and I were ready for a lunch break. But Peter showed no signs of slowing down. The Asian art gave him a second wind, and he stopped repeatedly, pointing out the beauty of diverse Chinese, Japanese, and Indian figurines and sculptures.

A full hour later we finally descended to the Staff Dining Room, situated underneath the Egyptian galleries. It caters to over 300 employees, and it is spacious and more comfortable than the public restaurant situated underneath the Medieval section. I still dearly miss the roomy old restaurant that was transformed into the Roman

Part Two

Court: its dim lights, fountain, plants, comfy plush chairs, the meals accompanied by a tuxedo clad pianist behind the grand piano playing a Mozart sonata, a Chopin nocturne, or a Jazz classic.

Over lunch I again prodded for personal tidbits in my vain endeavor to glean some morsels of information. I asked whether he'd ever returned to the former Czechoslovakia (present Slovak Republic). The question seemed to annoy him. "I've left that life behind me. I try to forget about it." He looked down, stabbed at the salad, before adding, "But, of course, I cannot forget."

Gradually, he shared some more of his past; about his father finally getting the papers that got him and his mother to the States, his reunion with his mother, who had miraculously survived Bergen-Belsen, and finally their reunion with his father in New York. I knew much of this from his book, but his firsthand account made it more immediate and direct. "Most of the books written about the Holocaust list all the names of family members that have died. I wrote about all those that survived." That was life affirming! For a while we continued eating in silence, and I didn't expect him to reveal much more, when he put down his knife and said, "Getting back to my Holocaust experiences; though I am now a well-adjusted individual – at least I think so – it is always with me under the surface of my consciousness. That does not mean that whenever I wake up, I think of the Holocaust, but if you do wake me up during the night and ask me for prisoner number, I will say 119,748 and go back to sleep. My wife once told me that I am obsessed by the Holocaust. I plead guilty to the charge." Martina, as a German, apologized to him for what the Germans had done to him. It's a guilt that many Germans share – surely one reason why the Germans were the most open to receiving Syrian and other refugees into their country. Peter kept chewing and didn't respond. It was much easier talking about art, which filled out the rest of the conversation.

As we sauntered toward the coatroom Peter couldn't resist stopping off at sundry galleries, coming alive again, finding his voice, pointing out this and that. Eventually we made it out of the museum and walked toward the busses. As soon as his bus arrived, he nudged my arm, flicked his hand in an offhand wave, and got on without another word. No goodbyes. We watched him walk down the aisle. He didn't turn around. As the bus disappeared into the traffic we strolled in silence through Central Park as far as the *Alice in Wonderland* sculpture before turning around.

We wondered whether we'd somehow offended him. He hadn't been that easy to read. Had I probed too much? Were we too Germanic? Had I not paid enough attention to his artistic explications? Had he expected something other from our meeting? We drove home in silence. I recalled the ending of his book, where he describes the moment of his parting with his two best friends from the concentration camps. His parting with Artur was especially poignant, underscored by the lack of ceremony. After all they'd gone through – sharing their meager meals, sleeping tightly together for warmth, and withstanding the daily horrors and abuse – they parted ways without a word, their realities deadened by the inhumane conditions they were exposed to, never knowing whether they'd survive another day. The way he'd just walked off into the bus reminded me of that. How much trauma was still unprocessed within him?

The enigma didn't leave me. I wanted to write to him – meaningful words, but the idea that we might have offended him in some way stayed with me. And I retraced my time with him, still trying to understand this 86-year-old man who had gone through such harrowing experiences, from which he clearly had not recovered, fully. He'd coped, made the best of his life, was successful, raised a family, got involved in his community, became a voluntary docent at the Met, wrote his memoir, gave talks on the Holocaust, traveled. Of course, no therapists, psychologists, or counselors were initially available for the survivors. They had to cope on their own. Most just never talked about their experiences. But we now know that for there to be any resolution, any closure, you have to tell your story, and name the hurt. Without that, as Desmond Tutu says so succinctly, it's difficult to move on, to forgive. In writing his book, *Memories of Evil,* he told his story and named the hurt. But that story needs to be told many times. At the bottom of all his emails he included: *never forget, never forgive.* The deeds are unforgettable, and should not be forgotten, so that they may serve as a reminder of what not to repeat. Looking at our current world situation, especially the Syrian Civil War, and the war with ISIS, I wonder if the world will ever learn. Forgiving? That's mysterious and personal. Forgiving is freeing, but it takes time.

When I had asked Peter how he came to love art so much he didn't give me a direct answer, just saying that he and his wife started going to galleries and museums on the weekends and never stopped. The love with which he approached every piece of art made me think that he'd found his therapy. Art became his solace. It made perfect sense that he particularly loved Asian art – art forms and traditions outside of Europe or the Western world – because it represented a mindset, a soul-scape, a spirit-steppe, far removed from his source of pain. But maybe I was reading too much into it, for he simply emphasized the art's overriding beauty, quoting Brancusi, "In the presence of an object of beauty, no explanations are necessary." Martina also noticed that he was particularly drawn to movement – little Chinese dancing sculptures or the dancing statues of India. He was especially effusive when he talked about Vishnu, Shiva, or Ganesha, relating their mythic stories. Or the tenderness with which he spoke about baby Krishna, suckled by the milkmaid Yashoda, as we stood in front of the small 12th century copper statue. Or how he explained the importance of karma and reincarnation, so integral to the Hindu worldview, to which Martina, in a subsequent email to him responded so aptly: *If one thought this consequently to the end, the people that wronged you and millions of others will find their reckoning on the path of Karma. So many have not been brought to justice in a way that would even get close to redeeming some of the evil committed, but nobody would be able to evade the universal, large, uncompromising laws of karma that will bring people and their deeds to justice over many life times to come. But nothing in this world will ever be able to make right what you had to suffer.* Was his immersion in Indian art helping him to re-align himself, to heal? I decided to wait a day before writing to Peter.

We Met at The Met

He beat me to it. He sent me an email stating how great it was to meet my wife and me at the Met, and he wished us a happy new year. So, I didn't have to feel bad after all. On the contrary, that same day he sent two more emails with photos of his family. I was touched by the gesture, and I said as much in my replies. However, late in the afternoon of December 24, as the sun was beginning to set, I received yet another email. In the subject line he wrote: *A Story*. And it was this very 'story' that put things in context. The story referred to the two boys he'd become friends with in the concentration camps, and their unceremonious parting. They'd been liberated on May 2nd, 1945, near the town of Schwerin in north Germany, after the harrowing 12 day 'Sachsenhausen Hunger March.' Kubicek paraphrased the wordless parting that he'd written about in his book: "We were not callous; we were not insensitive. We were simply emotionally dead. My entire concentration camp ordeal had felt surreal to me and thus Artur and Miki were equally unreal. Artur and I parted and we never saw each other again."

But 67 years later, his 'story' relates, he gets a telephone call from the daughter of Artur. When the daughter finds out that she had indeed contacted *the* Peter Kubicek, she put Artur on the phone and they talked again, communicating in rusty Slovak, a language they'd barely used since leaving. Artur informs Peter that Miki is also still alive living in Haifa. A few weeks later he gets a call from Miki. This phone-reunification had taken place in 2012. They remained in touch and he sent them both a copy of his book. Three friends reunited. In a manner of speaking they'd never really parted, bonded through the hell they were forced to endure. It was a timely and significant reconnection for shortly after Miki fell ill and died.

I waited a day before I responded, letting this story sink in. On December 25, I responded with the words:

A story of human relations! Poignant, uplifting, and profound. It made me think of the mysterious strands of destiny — the powerful connections we make with others. The conditions in which the three of you met were so dire and deadening, but something lived on, transcending time and space. That you were able to reconnect after almost seven decades is remarkable. It is life affirming — it is light in the darkness. It is revelatory. Thank you for sending that story. It certainly is thought provoking — deeply human. [...]

For a while I continued receiving regular emails from him, but over time they lessened and finally stopped. When December came around again, I found myself thinking about him again, wondering how he was faring. Finally, on December 22, exactly a year after our meeting at The Met, I decided to send him an email – attaching some photos of us that Martina had taken. A few days later his wife replied, informing me that he passed away on December 14th, adding, "The Met was one of his favorite pastimes. It's where he was happy and engaged, which is the way I like to remember Peter." I felt saddened, though I had only met him once.

Had his daughter not stopped by at my booth and bought *Meet Me at the Met* on that blustery and rainy day, I would never have had this significant encounter with this remarkable man and his extraordinary story. Experiences like that are worth more than any number of books sold.

Thumbing Down the Road

IF I WERE ASKED to design a crest symbolizing my adolescent years, I'd be tempted to include an outstretched arm and raised thumb as a central feature, though the thumbs-up gesture might delude people into thinking I was a happy, balanced and upbeat person, in harmony with my surroundings – which I unequivocally wasn't. On the contrary, those formative years included a painful hodgepodge of confusion, conflict, discord, discontent, self-doubt, and bitter loneliness. I rebelled furiously against the establishment, injustices, educational systems, societal-political norms and expectations, though my protests were mostly fueled by anger. That said, the open road was my escape route from all the proverbial teenage angst; it was my elusive key to relative liberty. In truth, the times I thumbed along the highways and byways belong to some of the happiest and most meaningful swaths of my life, even if it felt and appeared otherwise. While hitchhiking I got to know myself, others, and the world, albeit through a naively youthful lens. Those meandering roads merged into one vast gastrointestinal tract that helped me to digest the vagaries of life. And in retrospect, no matter where I went, I felt myself *trailing clouds of glory*. Viewed in that context the thumbs-up sign does coincide aptly with the symbol of the free and easy rider – if somewhat parasitic.

The first time was as uneventful as it was short-lived, though the measure of guilt I experienced of doing something sinful and illicit – like taking drugs, stealing, or cheating – more than made up for it. I was about twelve at the time, living in Empangeni, Zululand. A group of us were walking along the road when one

Part Two

of my friends suggested we hitchhike into town. Full of bravado, we stuck out our thumbs. To my relief, the cars passed us by. *You never know what kind of psychopath might pick you up.* We'd heard stories. The moment we spotted our 7th grade teacher, Mr. Botha, drive by on the other side of the road, we dropped our thumbs, hoping he hadn't seen us. He'd be sure to lecture us on the evils of the world, and possibly *cane* us on our buttocks to let his homily sink in. Safely out of sight, we started up again and seconds later a *bakkie* skidded to a stop. We whooped at the unexpected success – *it really works!* – and sprinted to the white pick-up truck. The father of a classmate who'd stopped for us shouted, "Hop on," and we scrambled into the back of the bakkie. Two minutes later he dropped us off at the town center, near the corner café: my maiden voyage with the humble help of my *digitus pollex* – the first of hundreds, maybe thousands.

I can't recall hitchhiking again till my fifteenth year: short innocuous trips to the movies, shopping malls, or to the occasional party in our immediate suburban surroundings in northern Johannesburg, mostly with a friend. That changed when I turned sixteen, responding to an inexplicable urge to get out and experience the world. From then on, hitchhiking became a serious mode of transportation. It coincided with my transferal from the local high school in Bryanston to Damelin College, a "cram-college" located in the center of Johannesburg. That alone felt liberating. I let my hair grow (in vindictive defiance to the short back and sides of public school), roamed around town during breaks and free periods, hung out in Wimpy Bars, record stores, or slipped into the Wellington Hotel across the road for a beer. Mostly, I took the bus, but as time went by, I began to hitchhike more often.

That summer I crossed the Rubicon and became a bona fide hitchhiker when I decided to thumb my way to the coast, instead of playing it safe and taking the train (a unique experience in its own right). My parents vehemently opposed my plan and forbade me to go, but the next morning – seeing my insistence – they acquiesced, and I departed, promising to call.

Blessed by beginner's luck, I caught a ride all the way to Durban with a salesman in a dusty grey Datsun, who barely uttered a word for the entire six-hour drive. That night I slept on the beach near Umhlanga Rocks, just north of *Durbs*. I woke up in the middle of the night hearing whispering voices nearby. Shadowy figures approached and chucked sand on my sleeping bag. I ignored them, but they inched closer and threw more sand. I had no idea who they were, and I already saw myself getting jumped. When another chunk of sand hit the lower side of my sleeping bag I instinctively leapt up and shouted, "Fuck the fuck off, before I *blerry bliksem* you! *Voetsak*, you hear!" putting on a heavy Afrikaans accent to sound more aggressive. Instantly, I regretted my impulsive outbreak, bracing for a pummeling. Instead, they retreated, mumbling, *Sorry man, we thought you were someone else*. Apart from that incident on the beach I remember little of that trip, merging as it did, with all the other hitchhiking trips through South Africa over the next five years.

Initially, my prime motivation was to get around for free, but with time I discovered that there's a whole ethos around hitchhiking, which increased in import the more I unfurled my thumb. The unknown became part of the thrill: Who's going to stop? How long will it take? How far can they take you? What kind of car, vehicle, or mode of transport will lift you to the next leg of your journey? Will it be comfortable? Safe? What conversations will emerge? What lessons learned? What hurdles overcome? Each trip became a pilgrimage of sorts. I went so far as to consider it a form of initiation, spiritual awakening, a rite of passage. Then again, I was and remain a romantic at heart. The open road was my holy land – *a la Sainte Terre* – and, in the alleged spirit of John Muir, I became a *Sainte Terre-er*, sauntering along the myriad roadsides with my magic thumb, instead of a hiking staff.

Part Two

The risk factor is ever present and all one can do is *Trust*. A friend of mine (drummer in a band I played in after the acrimonious breakup of Tokolosh), who'd missed his ride and hardly ever hitchhiked, was killed instantly when the car that had picked him up rolled over and crashed into a ditch close to his home. The driver got off unscathed. We've all had our close calls.

Once, I hitchhiked with my good friend Pierre through the Zulu highlands, when an Indian from Durban picked us up. He was in a foul mood, complaining about his job, his marriage, the apartheid system, the weather, and whatever his associative thinking chanced upon. And the more he vented, the faster he drove. Pierre and I looked at each other, not daring to utter a word. The winding roads through the steep hills narrowed, but instead of slowing down he took delight in swerving round the corners, the tires screeching, while his vitriol against the world escalated. To underscore his venomous remarks he lit a cigarette, puffed loudly, and stepped on the accelerator. We knew it was serious when he yelled, "What's the use of living? We're better off dead! Can't trust anybody." We held on tightly as he screeched through the hairpins. *Why had he even picked us up? Was it so he could release his ire openly? Get back at some white boys?* The sheer drop to my left appeared increasingly perilous as we sped up the mountain – certain death should the car plunge over the edge. Instead of slowing down after reaching the summit he accelerated, racing downhill toward the next bend in the road. The inevitable happened: the car slammed into the guardrail and spun into the opposite lane, tailspinning up onto the embankment, barely missing a tree. "Fuck-fuck-*fuuuuck*!" he screamed as if it were our fault. He swerved wildly and headed straight toward the next twist in the road. At the last moment he veered, skidded, and bashed into the guardrail. I thought we'd roll over, but miraculously he steadied the car, slammed on the brakes, came to a stop, and shouted, "Get out." We were only too happy to oblige. He didn't bother to assess the damage to his car, but sped off, the back-bumper dangling like a broken limb. As we traipsed along, we noticed that not all the hairpins had guardrails, and without them we wouldn't have survived.

Then there was the close call on one of my return tours to Jo'burg. I'd just met another hitchhiker who wanted to tag along for the rest of the trip, which tends to happen (not always welcome). It was a rainy day, and we stood under a bridge outside Laingsburg (Cape province), when a convoy of brand-new Isuzu pick-up trucks appeared. We stuck out our thumbs out of habit, not expecting that they'd stop, but to our surprise they did – all five. Never have so many vehicles stopped for me. The convoy was on its way to Johannesburg. The chances of ever getting a ride for a distance of over 700 miles are slim in the best of circumstances. What a lucky break. We'd be as good as home. All the African drivers were forthcoming and friendly, assuring us we'd help them stay awake if we joined them. The plan was to rotate from truck to truck every hour or so. I let my thumb-buddy choose with whom he wanted to ride first. He chose the pilot truck and I climbed into the truck right behind.

The rains worsened and the roads got increasingly slick. Yet, the lead car barely slowed down, which meant that the rest didn't slow down either. The loss of traction was obvious. On a number of occasions, I noticed the truck in front slipping and sliding precariously. "Did you see that?" I asked, hoping my driver would slow down, which he did, but only for a while, before speeding up again to catch up. Suddenly, the lead truck aquaplaned. In the driver's futile attempt to gain control, the truck swerved and spun off the road into a ditch, rolling over onto its roof. I feared the worst – blood spattered bodies slumped over and mangled in the cab. I couldn't help thinking that I'd almost sat in that truck. We all came to a skidding stop, jumped out, and ran to help. To our amazement they both clambered out the shattered windows unharmed, except for some minor scratches and bruises. The visibly shocked African who'd stopped for us, apologized profusely, urged us to move on, and implored us not tell anyone that they'd picked us up, least of all the police. I felt guilty and sorry for him and the others. Maybe nothing would have happened had they not stopped for us. We promised, bade them a glum farewell, and continued to walk down the rainy road till we lost sight of them. I cannot recall who picked us up next, but what I do recall is that we spent an uncomfortable night beside the road and that, on the following morning, as we scouted around for the most optimal place to stand, we came across a body lying in a shallow gulley. We both convinced ourselves that he was breathing, and not seeing any signs of violence, we left him there. In retrospect, we should have checked on him. Maybe he was wounded or sick, in need of help. And yes, maybe he was dead. Guilt in all shapes and sizes builds up over the years.

Close to a quarter of the rides I got in South Africa were in the back of a bakkie. I didn't mind. It saved me making conversation, and I could enjoy the scenery unimpeded – the smells, the temperature, and occasional cloudbursts. Some drivers picked up other hitchhikers on the way, which made for some jovial times, swapping stories of the road and exchanging travel tips. Sundry memories rise up of happy times sitting on the wheel-humps or standing up front, holding onto the bakkie's bulkhead, letting the warm winds rush through my hair and enjoying the landscape flitting by. On cold days I'd slip into my sleeping bag, hugged up against one of the sidewalls or wedged comfortably between other hitchhikers. I only recall one unpleasant bakkie ride.

It occurred while thumbing through the Swartkop Mountains. A slow moving bakkie stopped right next to me, saving me the usual run. As far as I can remember I have never rejected a ride (hard to believe), but I almost declined when I saw a newly slaughtered cow sprawled across the back of the pick-up truck, its legs dangling out the side and back. I couldn't spot a place to sit, except on the carcass, and the nauseating stench made me want to retch. Reluctantly I clambered on, my *tyre-tekkies* sullied and slipping in the coagulating blood. Moreover, it was chilly, uncomfortable, and each time the *Boer* turned a corner I had to steady myself, gripping onto the tail, the rope tied around its legs, or the bakkie's bloodied reinforced railings. Throughout the undulating drive my gaze kept returning to the dead cow's wide-eyed stare.

Over the years I've enjoyed all sorts of vehicles, though they were mostly run of the mill sedans, coupes, hatchbacks, station wagons, and other compact cars. Convertibles and super swanky models were a rarity, though it happened on occasion, such as when Pierre and I got a midnight ride in a Rolls Royce, or many years later when my future wife and I angled a luxury Bentley on our way up to London. Other vehicles also stick out, like when – on one of my numerous trips through the karoo – a black hearse stopped for me. The undertaker was on his way to a farm to collect the body, or so he said. It was a pleasant and comfortable trip, but there was something macabre about driving through the semi desert in a hearse with a coffin in the back. Part of me wondered whether there actually was a body in there already. And on a trip to Cape Town with my friend Fuzz (a bass guitarist with whom I often played music), an 18-wheeler stopped for us. The fatigued African truckdriver asked us to drive the rest of the way to Cape Town. Fuzz jumped at the opportunity, though he'd never driven such a massive semi before. "It's easy, the road goes on straight through the Karoo for hours," the truckdriver assured us (the Great and Little Karoo have played a major role in my hitchhiking ventures). "No bends, no turns, just straight. And instead of four, you have eight gears." With that he crawled into his sleeping cab behind the front seats and only reappeared when we arrived on the outskirts of Cape Town.

On another occasion, while on a camping trip in northern Zululand, a bus filled to capacity with rural Zulus stopped for us. The jovial driver and conductor tied our backpacks securely onto the roof, together with other precariously placed pieces of luggage, and invited us on board, free of charge. We joined the Zulus and a menagerie of goats, chickens and other livestock inside. No "white" bus would ever have done the same for a couple of young Africans during those apartheid days. It left a lasting impression of gratefulness. Then there were the odd rides on motorbikes, tractors, and yes, a squad car, though that doesn't count, because Pierre and I got picked up against our will – only to be dropped off beside the road like garbage after their futile search for drugs.

Though I did get a car when I was eighteen – a vintage 1964 cream colored VW bug – I still hitchhiked to the University of the Witwatersrand at least half the time, mainly to save on gas money. For a while I also got a motorbike (200hp Suzuki twin), but it was no fun winding my way through the congested morning traffic along Jan Smuts Avenue, and when it broke down and needed major repairs, I didn't bother to get it fixed. So, once again, I resorted to my fallback thumb.

It became a routine. I'd walk up to the top of Peter's Place (the road), stick out my thumb, and within minutes had a ride that more often than not shuttled me all the way to Wits. It was preferable, faster, and more interesting than the tedious bus rides. I had my regulars: There was the judge, who drove a spiffy Jag, who didn't say much, but had a sonorous voice and spoke with an English accent. I always wondered how many people he'd sentenced to death by hanging. During my freshman year a TA from the engineering department often gave me a ride. We laughed a lot and fell right into discussing a wide range of subjects from politics to literature to religion. I missed her when she graduated. For a while a taciturn psychology major with dark intense eyes picked me up. A voluminous moustache hid his pronounced cleft lip that revealed itself when he spoke, which was sporadic. The only thing I recall him saying was that he'd once lost his memory for three days. When it returned, he was lying naked and bloody on a beach, hundreds of miles from home. "Yup, never did find out what happened during those three days," adding after a lengthy pause, "Since then I've been watching myself go mad."

Then there was the bank clerk whose first words were, "I've just farted, so you'll want to roll down your window," lighting a cigarette to hide the smell. He turned out to be my most reliable ride. His dilapidated Toyota was littered with garbage and smelled of stale cigarette smoke, mold, and spoiled milk. Then, after almost two years, he didn't show up anymore. Months later, just before the end of my third year, he picked me up again. I barely recognized him. First off, he was driving a spiffy new BMW, and he'd permed his hair. In contrast to the inaugural day of the fart, the AC cooled car smelled fresh and new, with a waft of Old Spice aftershave – no trace of cigarette smoke. Not one soiled wrapper, pizza box, paper cup, girly magazine, or beer bottle anywhere. He even spoke differently: slower, softer, and with greater articulation. He wore a three-piece suit with a pressed shirt and golden cufflinks. He explained that he'd worked his way up in the company, saved money, and bought "This here BMW," lightly tapping the steering wheel. Furthermore, he'd married and was expecting. I still remember him saying, "I never thought I'd make it this far, but it goes to show what hard work and determination can do." He gave me a patronizing look. "Look where I am now," and he patted the steering wheel again, smiling smugly. "Maybe one day you can get to where I am now. You'll have to work hard. Remember that." He never stopped for me again, passing me by without the slightest sidelong glance, now that he'd stepped up in the ranks. Well, to this day there's still no BMW sitting in our driveway.

The waiting game! When I read, then saw Beckett's play, *Waiting for Godot*, I had to smile. I understood that play at its core and most basic level. Getting stuck in place for interminably long stretches of time – that's a huge slice of the thumber's life. Hitchhiking schools patience, willy-nilly. I am by nature an impatient person, always in edgy pursuit of purpose. Any impediments to my goals are cause for deep-set frustrations. Then again, the best things in life come with patience. Furthermore, you're never in full control, always at the mercy of chance or luck

– though providence plays a part, of that I am convinced. Be it as it may, waiting beside the road for that *god*damn car is part and parcel of the hitchhiker's waiting game; and there's no other way to see it – or treat it – but as a game (with benefits). Every time you hear or see a vehicle it's like the ever-elusive Godot sending signals that *he'll* appear, though he never does – just like those *Godotian* cars that never stop. Even a short wait can feel eternal, and one starts to have increasingly inane internal conversations like Vladimir and Estragon. I have often wondered how many hours of my life I've spent beside the road, waiting out the abominable stasis, experiencing the push and pull between serene acceptance and maddening frustrations. It's a constant tension that easily leads to inner conflict, let alone debilitating anxiety. But patience is a virtue, and letting go and practicing divine tolerance helps – as does singing; there's nothing like belting out a song in the middle of the *bundu*, with not a soul for miles around. We have to learn how to make light of that inescapable shadow. It accompanies us every time we stick out our thumb – our Siamese twin that easily turns into a predatory Doppelgänger. It's ever-present, no matter if the wait is short or long. Bottom line: we have to come to terms with waiting.

Twice I had to wait for longer than a day, and both those times occurred in the Great Karoo. The first time happened on my return journey with my friend Fuzz (who drove the 18-wheeler). We'd already spent one night next to the road in the semi desert terrain. By midday we were still stuck in the same spot. During the long wait he clued me up on the fundamental aspects of Buddhism. In turn I told him of the insights I'd gained through my studies of Madam Blavatsky, Theosophy, and Anthroposophy. In between we brewed Rooibos tea on the blue Cadac Cooker, ate stale bread, shared a milo bar, and counted ants. A bakkie did stop for us in the early afternoon. The farmer explained he was only going a few miles down the road, but we hopped on anyway, just to get a change of scenery. The place he dropped us off was indistinguishable from the previous spot, ants and all. More endless hours elapsed and we ate the last remnants of our meagre victuals. By now we wondered whether we'd ever get out of there. To pass the time we fantasized about the future, dreaming up outrageous scenarios of all the things we'd do, which turned into mawkish confessionals about our secret desires and the bad things we'd done, after which we lapsed into sullen silence. A quick but stunning sunset broke the monotony, though the cold and darkness set in almost immediately. When night descended around us, we could see the headlamps from miles away. Luckily, I usually wore a white shirt, so I stood in front of Fuzz and waved my arm to be noticed. We'd already resigned to spending the night beside the road when a Volkswagen Kombi stopped and a friendly young couple invited us on-board. From one moment to the next we'd stepped from the desolate, silent and empty Karoo into a party in full swing. Music blared; drinks, joints, and food made the rounds; and for the next few hours we became the best of friends with the other hitchhikers that lay sprawled in the back of the bus. For a night we became a likeminded fellowship of hitchhikers, something that I'd never experienced before nor would again. Eventually, we dozed off till we reached Johannesburg in the early morning hours. I think fondly of that night.

The second time took place during my first year at Wits University, exacerbated by the vow I'd taken to walk barefoot for a year. After watching the Zeffirelli's film *Brother Sun, Sister Moon*, about Saint Francis, I had decided to unfetter my feet in emulation of that compassionate Saint. Now, close to a year later, and during the three-week winter break in June/July I decided on a solo trip down to Cape Town – all barefoot. An unlucky star accompanied that trip. The first mishap ensued within the first hour. I got dropped off near the main highway, southwest of Johannesburg in proximity of Soweto Township, morning smoke rising from the shacks. As I walked toward the highway's entrance ramp I inadvertently stepped into a pile of broken glass. A piece got stuck in my left heel. In between waiting for cars, I tried to extract it with my pocketknife, but it only lodged itself more deeply. I gave up my useless attempt when a bakkie stopped for me. I hopped on, hoping the shard would naturally expel itself over time.

On the third day and about twenty cars later I reached Cape Town. At Clifton Beach, I bathed the gash and tried once more to pry the shard from the wound, but without success. Tired, despondent, and hungry I walked to the apartment of an old friend nearby who I wanted to look up. I had secretly hoped to stay with him for a few days. Hearing music, I knocked, opened the door, and shouted, "*Howzit* Daniel, guess what?" A pretty thirty something woman and her young daughter and son looked up at me from the sofa, taken aback by the sudden intrusion. I apologized profusely, hearing that he'd moved away months ago. Not knowing what else to do I hitchhiked to Sandy Bay near to Llandudno and hobbled along the narrow trail for about 20 minutes to the nudist beach where I wouldn't be arrested for vagrancy. I'd stayed there before (and would again). I kept to myself, convalesced, and after a couple of days felt fit enough to see if I could locate some of my other acquaintances from the time when I'd lived in Cape Town, but to no avail. So much for my plans to go clubbing, visit old haunts, discover different places, climb Table Mountain, and make new friends. But the weather was good and I enjoyed some relaxing hours on various beaches, frequenting cafes and looking over the ocean, my left heel throbbing throughout. At last I succumbed and hit the road home.

The return trip turned out to be even more miserable than the journey down: got soaked with heavy rains, slept in a trench and under a bridge in the Hex River Valley, and once again got stranded in the endless expanse of the Great Karoo, except this time it was winter. Not only was it a particularly cold midwinter's night, but the constant gusts of wind chilled me to the bone. At a forlorn and littered rest area I found a modicum of relief under some scraggly trees, blossoming with flapping plastic bags. The next morning at dawn I took up my position next to the road again, the flimsy blue sleeping bag wrapped tightly around my frozen feet. During that frigid night I decided, once and for all, that I'd had enough of going barefoot. I wasn't a Saint. I had nothing to prove, and – it must be said – almost a year had elapsed since the day I ceremoniously unfettered my feet in holy emulation. I'd kept my promise for the most part, but as yet, I was barefoot still and needed to get home.

It took another five hours before a young Boer with a crew cut on his way to Bloemfontein gave me a ride. To escape the boredom of the wait I started walking, mile merging into mile, the doppler effect of the passing cars and trucks feeding my melancholia. One car did stop, but when the man saw that I wasn't a luscious, voluptuous girl, he shouted, "Cut your *fokken* hair," speeding off with squealing tires, leaving me in a cloud of dirt and dust (not that that hadn't happened to me before or would again).

After that I flopped down on my backpack and no longer bothered to get up when cars appeared on the horizon. I just stuck out my thumb, halfheartedly. I was beyond caring, and didn't even notice that a car had not only stopped but was reversing toward me, saving me the run. The short unshaven man was visibly tipsy, but was heading straight for *Jozies*, which, in effect, would end my long wait. I did, however, wonder about my safety, since we still had over two hundred miles to go, and he kept swigging from his bottle of whisky, smoking one cigarette after another – Texan. And when the bottle was upended, he stopped and bought a bunch of tiny liquor bottles at a gas station, throwing them like candy on the dashboard. "Help yourself, my *china*." Though I wasn't much of a drinker I thought, what the heck, and downed a Smirnoff vodka, which dispelled my melancholia immediately.

His driving became progressively erratic the closer we got to Johannesburg. I offered to drive, but he simply laughed, shook his head, and wrung the neck of another micro bottle. He told me that he'd grown up on a farm in the Karoo and had just come from a family visit. "*Jy weet*, I was going to stay for two weeks, but after three days, *s'truths,* I got so *gatvol* bored… had to *waai* right out of there and get back to the city." Like him, I'd truncated my trip, but for different reasons. As we approached the city, he got increasingly excited. "See the smog over *Jozies*… it's a *regte* welcome home flag. Look at the skyline – it's like the arms of my *bokkie* reaching out to me, singing, 'come lie in my bed.' *Ag*, man, I love the smell of the city. I love its pollution. I *dinkum* do. It's like smelling the sweaty armpits of a woman, the swamp between her legs. That's what I'm going to enjoy tonight. Can you smell it?" and he snatched the last of the little variegated bottles.

That evening, when I eventually made it home, I extracted the glass shard with the help of a box cutter and pincers, wondering whether the trip had been a colossal waste of time. No, if nothing else, I'd had an indelible self-confrontation. On the road, we are thrust together with people we otherwise would never meet or choose to be with. That much is clear. In short, more than getting around, it's about the people we meet on the way – a pertinent metaphor for life. It's about the intriguing diversity of humanity. And we meet all sorts, good and bad, though in my experience, the good hold sway.

Apart from waiting, the situation often demands as much time hiking as hitching, like when people dropped me off on the outskirts of a town or far from my destination. Or I simply got bored with waiting around and moved on just to get a change of scene. A representative incident happened early on in my hitchhiking days after a sharp confrontation with my high school English teacher who had the audacity to cut my hair for circumventing Damelin College's hair regulations. Nowadays I could have sued him. Though we could grow our hair longer than in public schools, it could not go beyond the collar. I had evaded the issue by curling my hair to make it appear shorter, but was finally caught out at a random hair inspection. "What have we here?" he'd asked sarcastically, unfurling my hair, after which he sent me to his office where he grabbed a pair of scissors and butchered my locks. Needless to say, I walked right out of school, caught the next bus home, packed my backpack and hitchhiked to Tonquani Gorge in the Magaliesberg, where I stayed the night in the company of a troop of noisy baboons. On my long walk back along the twenty-mile dirt road, I didn't even hear or see a car, except for a brief glimpse of a tractor turning into a driveway. I passed the time reading *Catcher in the Rye*, identifying with Holden Caulfield, the protagonist, especially against the backdrop of having had my hair chopped off by a person of authority – a teacher who should have been a role model. That was the first time I spent more time hiking than hitching. From then on walking became standard practice, which also relieved the tedium of waiting.

Another time, one late afternoon, having found an appropriate place to stand at a crossroads outside a town somewhere in the Cape Province, a group of young brightly dressed "coloured" girls and women walked by. As soon as they saw me, they warned me that the men would soon be returning home from work and if they'd see me, they'd not only rob me, but beat me up, maybe even kill me. "Keep moving as far and fast as you can from here, because you're standing at the crossroads to the township," and they pointed down the dirt road that forked off the main road. "You'd better hurry." I saw real concern in their eyes. I immediately followed their advice, putting as much distance between me and the "coloured" township as possible, walking till a car finally stopped for me. I've never forgotten those women, sent by Hecate, Goddess of crossroads to protect me. I'm a firm believer that hitchhikers have a deity that takes care of them.

Over time I'd devised a little game, which I mostly only played late at night when I was desperate. After hours of waiting, I would set myself a limit: *If I'm not picked up by the tenth car I will give up and sleep beside the road.* An then I'd count – one set of approaching headlamps after the other. This method worked for me on numerous occasions, which has underscored my belief in the hitchhiker's deity, the one who protects and cares for the ride-angling rambler, confirmed by the number of times the tenth and last car stopped for me. Granted, sometimes I did extend it to fifteen or twenty cars. Nonetheless, I did have to sleep in a ditch or under a bridge a few times.

When I hitchhiked to and fro between Randburg and Johannesburg, I generally made it in two or three stops (unless I got rides with my regulars to Wits University). The first, starting from Bryanston, took me along William Nicol Drive to Hyde Park Corner (a small but cozy little shopping mall); then down Jan Smuts Avenue to Rosebank; and from there past Zoo Lake to Wits or the center of Johannesburg. I must have done that trip hundreds of times. Apart from going to Wits, there were the trips to Hillbrow or downtown to the Carlton Center, which was *the* place to go to in the seventies. Clubs, bars, movies, eating out, concerts, ice-skating, or just hanging out – there was always a good reason to head into town. Those trips were mostly uneventful, but a few stand out.

While standing at my usual corner in Rosebank, a decrepit rusty black sportscar stopped for me. The front passenger seat was loose and whenever he accelerated or put on the breaks I shot back or forth, forcing me to grab onto the sides.

After that kinetic introduction he asked, "Where to?"

"Hillbrow."

"Hillbrow, huh?" He paused, stepped on the gas, causing me to lurch back. "Do you take drugs?" I hesitated, not knowing whether he wanted me to say yes or no. He had scraggly oily hair, wore a stained and shabby leather jacket over a torn t-shirt, and his jeans were faded. I decided on *no*, not wanting to get involved in any kind of drug consumption with him, not that I partook much of anything. "So, you don't have any drugs on you."

"No, nothing," and to make myself clear, I said, "I'm not into that sort of thing."

"Well, you're lucky, because otherwise I'd have arrested and clobbered you, *eksé*. You know why the seat is broken?" and to emphasize his question he slammed on the breaks so that I slid forward into the dashboard, saved only by my quick reaction.

"No, why?"

"Because last night I whacked the guy so hard that it broke the seat – and his nose. He was stoned out of his mind, so he didn't feel much, but he's hurting now," and he laughed. "I'm an undercover narcotics officer. I clean up Hillbrow, but it's a losing battle. It makes me so *kwaai,* that I *fokken* have to *donner* them. They *blerry* deserve it." He gave me a sideways glance. "You look like you take drugs."

"I know. It's annoying. I hate being labelled." He dropped me off near the Hillbrow Tower.

At another time, I was hitchhiking at the same place in Rosebank when a biker walked up to me in full "Grim Reapers" regalia. His bike had broken down and he had to get to town. "Can I join you?" I wasn't going to say 'no.' "Hey, look at my tattoo."

"Wow, what happened?"

"Got fucken infected." He laughed. "But she's crazy sexy. Check her out. She's my *cherry*," and he pointed to the curvy big-boobed beauty squatting naked on a motorbike, her curvaceous booty popping into the sky, her long hair streaming in the wind. He flexed his arms so that she appeared to move. But his upper arm was red and swollen. Yellow goo and puss oozed from her orifices, breasts and hair. "She's got a bad case of syphilis," and he laughed at his own joke.

"You should get that seen to."

"For sure. Today… so, how long before we get a ride?"

"Depends, a few minutes, but never more than half an hour."

"That long! Fuck. I don't do this hitchhiking shit, but I crashed my bike two days ago, totaled." At that moment two other hitchhikers stuck out their thumbs up the road from us. "Hey, they'll get a ride before us. Let's go and fuck those two *poepols* up." I had no desire to get into a fight. Besides, they looked really friendly.

"This is a much better place. Trust me. I stand here all the time. They're standing just below the *robots*. Nobody wants to stop again when they turn green, and besides, there's no good place to stop. Down here the road widens." At that moment the lights turned green and two lanes of cars rushed forward, passing them by – and us.

"Why don't the fuckers stop," and he flipped off the cars and shouted, "Go fuck yourselves." At that moment a car sped through the yellow light, passed the other two but screeched to a halt for us.

"See, told you," I said, more relieved than triumphant. I jumped out early in Braamfontein to escape his company.

Indeed, you meet all types while hitchhiking but some people stick to you like burs. South of Durban on my way down the coast I met a guy heading for Margate. Over his baggy green dungarees, he wore a vintage British army trench coat, which made him look even more massive than he was. He had a round freckled face with a tousled beard, wispy hair, and a perpetual smile. And he talked incessantly. After an exhausting hour on the road with him I knew I had to get away from him, fast. He, on the other hand, took a fancy to me. As we reached Port Shepstone, I told him that I was actually going to Plettenberg Bay and not to Margate.

"*Kiff*, I'll come with you. I've always wanted to go there." I should have known.

"You know that we'd have to hitchhike all the way through the Trasnskei, yes? It could take days."

"Who cares." He shrugged and laughed. "I've got time. And don't worry, I'll look after you," and he whisked out a pair of nunchakus and began to twirl them around at a tremendous speed and too close to my head for comfort. "I've watched every Bruce Lee film many times over. I can use these fuckers," and he whacked a nearby STOP sign, leaving a dent in the center of the letter O. "Nobody messes with me. Some have tried... they'll never walk the same again. I've got another pair and can use them both together," and he whacked the STOP sign again in fast succession, making the battered O look like a grimacing smiley face. "So, Plettenberg Bay? Cool" So much for my attempt to get rid of him.

We got to Kokstad with ease, but only made it to Umtata by sundown. No use to continue hitchhiking at such a late hour. I recalled the comfortable night I'd spent at the Royal Hotel the first time I'd passed through Umtata and the Transkei when we moved from Cape Town to Empangeni. Had I been alone I would have splurged and stayed there the night, for old time's sake. But Nunchaku Man had barely any money and I had already paid for a liter of milk, jam donuts, and a few strips of biltong that he just plonked on the counter.

"We'll sleep at the Police Station," he said. "I've done it before. Come on." I'd also done it before, the time Pierre and I had hitchhiked back from our memorable trip to Blyde River Canyon, in northeastern South Africa. Though the canyon is spectacular, I didn't have good memories of staying at the police station in Lydenberg, mainly because I'd suffered through the worst case of diarrhea ever, without the benefit of a toilet in our cell. Nonetheless, I tagged along, swayed by the big man's enthusiasm. It worked. We got a cell, though it only had one bed (and no toilet). "First dibs," and he flung himself down on the creaky mattress. I made do on the hard cement floor, wondering whether it wouldn't have been better to spend the night in a ditch.

Next morning, we got a ride in a Chrysler Valiant, filled with other Africans on their way to work. They didn't seem to mind making room for two more white boys. The driver, as huge as Nunchaku Man, had the aura of a chief. I offered him some money, but he declined. He dropped us off in a beautiful area of the Transkei, with rolling hills all around. I don't recall the other cars that picked us up, but I do recall hours spent beside

Part Two

the road with him trying to teach me how to use the nunchakus, which resulted in me getting bruised all over to the delight of Big Boy. Once we'd reached Plettenburg Bay, I hoped that he'd finally move on. I said that I was going to get a room at a bed and breakfast, explaining that I didn't have enough money for the two of us. He accompanied me anyway, and when he found out that they charged by the room and not the number of people, he joined me. He wasn't so stupid after all. I inquired discreetly what his plans were after Plettenberg Bay and he said that he'd go back home to Pietermaritzburg, inviting me to join him. I declined and the next afternoon I bade him farewell.

"I thought we'd stay here for a few days."

"Changed my mind.

"So, where are we going?"

"Not we. Me!" I was miffed. "You're going home to Pietermaritzburg, and I'm... well, I'm not sure, but I'll most likely head south along the Garden Route for a while, maybe all the way to Cape Town.

"Sounds like fun. You're in luck. I don't need to be back home yet. I'll just join you." To my chagrin he joined me all the way to Cape Town, and I had to continue putting up with his constant jabbering, his silly ideas, his nunchakus that kept whirling around my head, and the loud childish laughter. In Cape Town we made for Sandy Bay again, which delighted him, immediately doffing all his clothes and jumping into the waves. Spotting some seals at the far end of the Bay he returned and said: "I'm going to clobber a seal. Want to come?"

"You can't do that! Not in front of all these people. It's cruel."

"So what! It's only a seal. And I don't have to kill it, just whack it a few times. Practice my nunchaku skills."

"Okay, you do that. I'll just hang out here."

"And why are you still dressed? You gotta get in the nude, dude." The naked giant laughed at his own rhyme and trotted off, swinging his nunchakus, while checking out the naked chicks.

After ten pulsing seconds, I jumped to my feet, grabbed my backpack and ran off up the trail. Before turning the corner, I looked back. The seals had already swum out into the ocean as Big Pink stood walloping the incoming waves with his nunchakus. There was something pathetic in the sight, and I felt sorry for him on some level. I hitched a ride into Cape Town and straight onto the N1. It was eerily reminiscent to my previous departure from Cape Town, only that I didn't have a glass shard stuck in my foot anymore. I would have stayed a few more days in Cape Town, but I wasn't going to risk crossing paths with Nunchaku Man again.

One gets an almost clairvoyant ability to "read the cars": what kind of vehicles will or won't stop. It's a given that Government vehicle will pass you by (unless the police apprehend you for vagrancy or on suspicion of carrying drugs). The same holds true for swanky Mercedes roadsters, E-type Jags, Porsches, or other luxury models (young pretty women have told me otherwise). Company cars, older couples, families, are still infrequent stoppers, but you never know. Your appearance and who you are makes a difference too. Because of my long hair I had more trouble than the ubiquitous army recruits with their duffel bags, desperate to get home for their weekend pass. Whenever I saw one of these national service peeps, I patiently stepped aside, knowing that I'd only have to wait a few minutes before someone would stop to give them a lift. No use competing with them. Everybody wants to pick up a *troepie*. Yet, I looked quite harmless – as some people told me when they picked me up, though I wondered whether to take that as a compliment or not.

It became a habit to peer at the initials on the number plates, depending where I was headed and where I stood. The first letter stood for the province: N for Natal, O for Orange Free State, T for Transvaal, and C for the Cape. Thus, ND stood for Durban, NUF for Empangeni (Natal, Umfolosi), NZ for Mtunzini, NP for Pietermaritzburg, OB for Bloemfontein, TJ for Johannesburg, CA for Cape Town, and so on (of, course that's all changed now).

Part Two

If you were trying to get to Johannesburg and you were standing outside Lydenburg in the Transvaal, you'd basically ignore the TAE (Lydenburg) number plates and focus on the TJ plates. Or alternatively, you could write the initials of your destination on a piece of cardboard, such as "TJ," something I rarely did, because it could potentially limit the number of cars that might stop for you.

For the most part I was a decent denizen of the road. Once, however, while hitching in the Free State, a convoy of army trucks passed me by. I didn't bother to stick out my thumb, and just remained perched on my backpack. The last truck, filled with recruits, started jeering at me, calling me a long-haired hippy, *poesie papgat, moffie*, and other nasty things. On impulse, I got up and flipped them off, igniting an immediate and explosive roar of cumulative anger, some jumping up, and others banging on the window for the driver to stop. *What the fuck have I just done!* I thought to myself, looking around and realizing there was no place to hide – nothing but a wild expanse of dry, flat grassland. Besides, they'd outrun me within seconds. I resigned and braced myself for a vicious beating. Unbelievably, the brown army truck just kept going, most likely not wanting to be left behind in the convoy. I was so thankful that I almost flipped them off again in triumph, but refrained from tempting fate.

Minutes later, an archeologist who'd studied at Wits University stopped and gave me a ride in his white Kombi Bus for a few hundred miles. He was listening to a tape of Leonard Cohen and began to tell me all about that Canadian poet and singer-songwriter, which helped me to regain my inner equilibrium after that close encounter with the SADF – South African Defense Force. There was something immensely comforting about listening to the soothing and sweetly melancholic songs, while attending to the soft-spoken archeologist expound on their meanings. To this day, whenever I hear or listen to "Hallelujah," "Suzanne," or "So Long, Marianne," I also have to think of him.

Thumbing Down the Road

When I finally got my military call up papers and could no longer defer my national service, I decided to take one last trip before skipping the country. That summer, early December, I hitched down to Port Edward, south of Margate, where I met up with James and his girlfriend, Jane, with whom I'd studied at Wits University. Every part of that trip was a moment of farewell. I even took pleasure in the prolonged waiting periods along the road. The three of us hiked the approximately hundred miles south to Port St. Johns. Jane had somehow lost her shoes, and in empathy with her, Keith and I unfettered our feet and walked the entire stretch barefoot, something I was used to after my year sans shoes. Most of it was along the beach, though we braved rain, rocky territory, and murky rivers – uniting with nature and the unique mood of the coastal Transkei, conscious, all the while, that I most likely wouldn't set foot on African soil for many years to come. Arriving in Port St. Johns about ten days later, we stayed the night in the local hotel before parting ways.

I took the bus north to Lusikisiki (the only white person) from where I hitchhiked back to Port Edward, up to Durban, and inland to Johannesburg. It went relatively smoothly, except when four guys, drunk and stoned out of their minds, picked me up near Ladysmith. The car was a "hothouse" of intoxicating fumes, and I got high just sitting there. They lit up one joint after another (Durban Poisons), laughing, roaring, and singing off-key throughout, while passing bottles of whisky, gin, and beer around, all of which I refused. They didn't hold it against me, but their erratic driving through the mountainous terrain worried me. Luckily, an unexpected traffic jam, forced them to slow down. *Traffic jam, out here in the bundu?* As we crawled along and rounded a corner, lights flashed. "Fuck! Cops," the driver shouted, coming to a stop. "Snuff the *zols*, hide the *dagga*, stack away the booze." I already saw myself busted for drugs. As we waited, one of them got out to investigate. He returned, quipping, "No worries, they're just looking for someone." It didn't change the fact that the car was stashed with illicit *stuff*, and that they were clearly wasted, including myself to some degree. When we finally reached the cops, they peered through the window and waved us on without a second thought. Farther on, we passed a group of Africans, handcuffed and huddled together beside the road, guarded by more cops. I felt sorry for them, wondering what they'd done, if anything. Had we been black, they'd have arrested us for possession of illegal drugs and driving while intoxicated. Apartheid was alive and well.

Feeling nauseous, I made some lame excuse to be dropped off at the next intersection. They obliged and roared off. For a long while I stood alone and motionless on the deserted road, relishing the tremendous stillness all around. Gradually, I lifted my head and stared up at the starry southern sky. The light of the half-moon augmented the magnitude of the mountainous region around me. The silence and fresh mountain air stood in stark contrast to the frenetic hour spent in the fumes of the toxic hothouse car. As I peered up into the night, recognizing the ever-reliable constellations, I felt my soul responding to its creative power, and I was overcome by a rare sense of comfort and self that I'd never experienced before – a liberating epiphanic moment where I realized I was indeed a microcosm of the all-encompassing macrocosm. Instead of feeling like a dust mite in the vast expanse of the firmament, I felt my entire being as an integral part of the *All*.

I experienced that nocturnal moment – standing there alone on the road between the coastal lowlands and the interior highlands – like a baptism of my fledgling *Self*. I was 21 at the time and my life was about to change irrevocably. I did not expect anybody to pick me up at this late hour, stuck in the middle of the escarpment to the highveld, but somebody did, and I made it back home. That ended my last tour before I absconded to Europe.

During the first few months in Basel, Switzerland, I didn't hitchhike at all. My foremost focus was to get an apartment, find a job, make money, and get acclimatized. Besides, the public transport system was excellent. Soon enough, however, I resorted to thumbing around locally. The first major hitchhiking trip happened on impulse.

More than a year had passed and I'd moved to the Black Forest, Germany. That summer I hopped on a train to pick grapes in Southern France. However, arriving in the Cotes de Provence wine region where I'd planned to meet a friend, I discovered that I'd lost the exact address of the vineyard. Without my friend, the idea of working on a vineyard lost its appeal, though I had no desire to return home immediately. The warm and inviting Mediterranean stirred my sense of adventure and I decided to take advantage of the situation and hitchhike along the coast all the way to Portugal. Besides, I'd saved some money to keep me afloat for a few weeks, and I'd only wanted to work on the vineyard to get to know the girl I'd met while still living in Basel.

While spending the night in the park in St. Tropez, I met up with a short and stocky hitchhiker from Canada with black unkempt hair, who sported a large Canadian Maple Leaf and a lightning bolt Kiss logo on his backpack. He was a "Hey Dude" kind of guy, relishing his first trip through Europe, eager to "taste" the mademoiselles. He wore tight fitting faded jeans with a metal studded black belt. He'd discovered Gauloises cigarettes, and every time he lit up, he'd spread his legs, take a match and strike it on his zipper, singing, "Come on baby, light my fire." We thumbed along the coast for a couple of days before we split ways somewhere around Toulon or Cassis.

Shortly after, just beyond Marseilles, a German in a corroded green Volvo stopped. "Where are you going?" he asked.

"Don't know, maybe Portugal. You?"

"Don't know, maybe Portugal."

"Great." In that moment we'd made a tacit agreement to travel together and I offered to help pay for some of the gas. Henning and I were the same age, had a lot in common, never running out of topics to talk about. He had a small cosmetics case full of cassette tapes, and introduced me to the music of German musicians and bands such Udo Lindenberg, Konstantin Wecker, Grobschnitt, Amon Düül, Can, Steinwolke, Guru Guru, and many more. I'd heard of some of the bands, but had never listened to them extensively. Of course, he also had a many other British and American bands, all of which added to the backdrop of that trip.

We drove over the Pyrenees through Andorra: the micro European state with impressively steep valleys and ravines. Entering Spain was like stepping into another century or returning to a past incarnation – initially, at any rate. We first stopped off at a little medieval village growing out of the flat expansive terrain like a coral reef, the narrow alleys strung with flapping laundry.

We barely stopped in Barcelona, deciding we'd sightsee on our return journey, which didn't end up happening (I still haven't made up for that loss). Instead, we searched for remote places, mostly secluded beaches, where we cooked meals on his primitive cooker and brewed strong black coffee.

In Cartagena, while exploring the surroundings, we mistakenly drove into an army zone. Suddenly we heard shots, the bullets zooming over our heads in fast succession. Clearly, the army recruits took vindictive pleasure in shooting at us. As we sped off, they must have shot a cannon or some sort of 'big gun' in our direction because we not only heard the huge boom, but felt it whizz just above our car, causing it to shake.

That night, Henning was determined to get someone to buy us drinks. We went to one of the lively port restaurants and found a seat outside. Trying but failing dismally as a conman, Henning finally found a heavyset balding man who seemed lonely and in need of company. He welcomed our friendly overtures, though Henning only wanted to cajole some free drinks out of him. Henning complimented him on everything: "Ah wow, great; yeah, that's so cool; hey; I really like your leather jacket; are you here on vacation?" He wasn't making much headway, but he persisted.

"You look like you're famous? I think I've seen you before, but I don't know where."

"Really?" and he lit up. "Maybe it's because of this," and he pulled out a very tattered piece of paper. He unfolded it as if it was a precious document. "Look, it's me in a Jägermeister ad. You know the ones that appear on the back pages of magazines – a new one every week." And indeed, there he was (looking much younger), holding a green Jägermeister bottle, with a toothy pinched smile and the ubiquitous statement underneath, starting with the words, *Ich trinke Jägermeister, weil...*"

"That's it. That's where I must have seen you. It's from the *Eines für alle* campaign. Hey, you should order a round of Jägermeister for us all, so we can say we've had a drink with a person who actually appeared in one of those ads." And, against my expectations, he did just that, and we toasted each other with a raucous "Eines für alle," downing the incredibly bitter herbal schnapps in one go. Henning didn't try out his con skills again after that.

Leisurely we drove along the coast, stopping here and there, meeting people, frolicking in the ocean, frequenting cafes and nightclubs, walking through towns and villages, eating out or cooking our own food. We slept mostly on the beach, but sometimes in the car. He'd sleep across the front seat (he insisted) and I curled up in the more comfortable back. That first night in the car I woke up to him shouting, "It's mine, get away... don't steal my stuff. No, no, stop..." followed by unintelligible words. I sat up, wide awake, perplexed and anxious as to how this raving rant would play out. What had happened? Had someone tried to break in? I couldn't see or hear anybody. Henning thrashed about as if warding off an attacker. Midst his ravings he bent down, retrieved a steel cash box from underneath the front seat, opened it, and fingered the bills, mumbling, "Still there, good, good." He closed the box, placed it back under the seat and settled down again.

Part Two

"Do you ever talk in your sleep?" I asked him the next morning.

"Did I do that again?" and he laughed. "What did I say or do this time?"

"Don't worry, I won't steal your money," and I told him what I'd witnessed. "I was worried that you'd beat me up, really."

"I'm sorry, I remember nothing. Really." From then on, I ignored his mumblings and occasional ravings.

At a small place called Los Lobos, a few hours southwest of Cartagena, we realized we'd never make it to Portugal. Our money had eddied away. To mark our defeat, we bought a bottle of whisky at a trading store and drowned our disappointment right there and then. Within seconds our joint melancholia gave way to – *what, me worry?*

Realistically, with the money available, we wouldn't even make it back home. We'd underestimated the cost of gas. "We'll have to syphon off some gas from other cars," Henning suggested.

"We can't do that. That's stealing."

"Do you have a better idea?"

"Let's just see how far we get. Maybe it'll be okay."

"Doubt it."

We drove through the night, aiming to return to Germany as fast as possible. "Give me all your money," Henning said, driving off the highway late one night into a gas station. He counted all the money. "Well, with our combined funds we'll get about half a tank." He got out, adding, "You drive, I'm tired." Shifting over into the driver's seat I waited for him to fuel up.

Minutes later he dashed back in, slammed the door and shouted, "Drive, quick. Drive!"

"Don't you have to go in and pay first?"

"Go, go, go," and he punched me on the shoulder. I fumbled with the keys, trying to get it started. "Come on, let's get out of here." The Volvo roared to life. "Step on it!" I pressed my foot down hard and we burned right out of there, tires screeching, the attendant running out screaming in our wake. "Faster, faster."

Back on the highway, Henning yelled, "Now get off at the first exit." Veering off we drove along byways parallel to the highway for about twenty miles.

"Okay, I think we're good." I didn't feel too guilty, admitting that I rather enjoyed the adrenalin rush of our movie-style getaway. "Let's find a place to rest for a couple of hours before moving on. Though we had a full tank of gas it still wouldn't get us back to Germany.

By the time we arrived in Barcelona, we were down to a few pesetas. Enough for one last meagre meal. Henning suggested we go to the German or Swiss consulate. He'd heard that they sometimes help people out. *Why not?* At the Swiss consulate, I showed them my passport, explained our predicament (with Henning adding something about being robbed), and to my surprise, they handed me 200 Swiss francs worth of pesetas, no questions asked, except my word that I would pay the money back on our return. We promptly celebrated our success at the nearest restaurant, before returning to Germany. He drove me all the way back to Villingen-Schwenningen where I lived. Good old Henning.

During my time in Germany I played in a rock band: Tokolosh (without an E). We had dreams of stardom, composed, performed, recorded, accumulated huge debts, broke up, went bankrupt. During that long two-year stint, I hitched a lot – mostly local. I never did buy a car, spending all my money on equipment and recording costs. For sanity's sake, I had to escape the Black Forest confines every few months: Italy, Greece, England, France, and that aforementioned trip to Spain with Henning. These trips were a combination of trains, busses, and some hitchhiking. The more money I earned the less I hitched, and truth be told, the thrill was gone. I didn't plan any hitchhiking trips anymore, got increasingly impatient with the vagaries of the road, and only resorted to the thumb out of necessity. It became a burden. I got tired of the endless waiting, the running up to cars, the tediousness of making conversation, the mostly silent rides with people with whom I had little to nothing in common, or having to listen to the incessant *yakkety-yak* of bored drivers. Though I still felt grateful, most rides were bland and uneventful. Nevertheless, a couple did stand out, such as the incident with the midges, up in Scotland.

Nobody was going to give us a ride anymore, that much was clear. Dusk slumped around us and the road yawned empty. No hotel for miles around, and we'd already walked for almost two hours, hoping to come across a bed and breakfast. We hadn't intended to hitchhike (my partner at the time did not approve), but we'd missed the last bus to Iona. As we trudged past one of the few houses beside the road, a beagle, attached by a short black leash to an elderly white-haired lady, interrupted his evening sniff to yap at us. Out of resigned desperation, I asked her whether we could camp in her yard.

"I suppose you can." She paused, scrutinizing us. "But aren't you worried about the midges?"

"No, we'll be fine. Thank you." I'd understood "*midgets*," which I naïvely interpreted as little humanoid folkloric creatures like the dwarfs in fairytales – a rather endearing concept. No sooner had we begun pitching our tent when the full import of her innocuous question became abominably clear. Swarms of the miniscule monsters appeared from nowhere, impeding our efforts to erect the tent at every turn. Our sorry shelter made for a flimsy and futile refuge. In fact, it increased their desire to feast on us, because they got attracted to the carbon dioxide in our breath like moths to light, something I only found out much later. The tent was like a greenhouse of carbon dioxide.

We couldn't escape the marauding mass. Killing the infinitesimal beasts was useless, and – as it turned out – so was everything else. They always found a way to feast on our flesh, suck our blood, inflicting severe pain. Susie took out cigarettes to smoke the critters out. I lit my pipe. The smoke simply excited them and the black plague continued – hour after hour after hour. We wrapped ourselves up entirely in our sleeping bags – to no avail. Throughout that sleepless night we endured the burning stings. Feeling like boiled lobsters we broke camp before dawn and set off down the cold dark road. Walking offered some relief, but no sooner did we stop for even two seconds, when a new wave of the dreaded pest engulfed us. "Just keep walking," I muttered. Susie was close to tears.

We were on the Isle of Mull and had hoped to reach Iona the previous night. We'd bought a Brit-rail Pass, but, of course, there were no trains to Iona. So far, we'd visited Stonehenge, Tintagel in Cornwell, and Wales, where I had intended to visit the stone circle at Penmaenmawr. However, after a cold and rainy night, Susie had rebelled, insisting we abort that part of the trip. Instead, we traveled on to Stratford-upon-Avon to pay homage to Shakespeare, after which we trundled on to the Lake District to honor Wordsworth, hitching the last part to picturesque Lake Windermere. While exploring the surroundings, we did chance upon a serene stone circle, which made up for the missed cromlech near Penmaenmawr. Then, after a short stopover in the walled medieval town of York, we headed toward Oban and sailed over to the isle of Mull, between mist veiled anthropomorphic rocks that jutted out of the mirror calm waters. What we should then have done is checked into a Bed & Breakfast at Craignure and taken the bus the following day. My fault.

Instead, we'd spent a sleepless night with the ferocious and ravenous midges and were now tramping along this deserted road, with about another twenty miles to go. After an hour, a tractor stopped for us. We could have hugged the farmer for his kindness. He dropped us off at the bus stop, saying that no bus would stop for us otherwise.

Though we must have made a smelly and sorry sight as we got on the bus, we felt elated to be rescued from our plight. After a short wait at Fionnphort, we boarded a small, red ferry that took us and a few others over to Iona. As we approached the green and rocky isle, the previous night's anguish dissolved and gave way to bliss, for me at any rate. "Let's go get a bite to eat, shall we?" I suggested as we disembarked at St. Ronan's Bay. It wasn't much of a restaurant, but some hot coffee and a toasted cheese sandwich amounted to a feast. Though our episode with the midges marked the nadir of our trip through the British Isles, Iona proved to be the zenith. Not much happened outwardly, but the mood and quality of that mystical and mythical isle entered into every pore of my being, allowing me to return inwardly to that hallowed place whenever the inclination arises. Needless to say, Susie and I broke up shortly after that trip.

The last major hitchhiking tour happened unplanned. A few weeks before departing for Emerson College in England, I'd decided, on a whim, to visit a girlfriend in Geneva. I was living back in Basel (after the demise of Tokolosh) and decided to hitchhike, instead of taking the train. Somehow, the rides took me off track and I found myself navigating the byways through Switzerland, arriving in Geneva after sunset. Unfortunately, we quarreled, and I ended up spending the night underneath an upturned boat next to Lake Geneva. The next morning, instead of going back to Basel, I hitchhiked to the South of France, catching a ride with a Frenchman who spoke no English or German (or chose not to). He sped along the autoroute at over 200 km/h, only slowing down at the tolls, dropping me off on the outskirts of Marseilles. That evening I was comfortably ensconced in a medieval and beautiful coastal town near the Spanish border, still smarting from the painful parting. The next day, I suffered a fall while climbing up a stone wall, twisting and bruising my foot and heel: a fitting metaphor to my break up. I stayed two more days, sleeping on the beach and bathing my throbbing foot in the Mediterranean Sea. Once again, I aborted a trip and started to hitchhike home.

With all my ill luck on that tour, I did have some truly uncanny good luck. Not initially, though. After a long wait I finally decided to play my countdown game – to hold out for another 20 cars before catching a train back to Basel. No sooner thought than a green VW Kombi Bus stopped for me and ferried me all the way to Basel (yet another Kombi Bus savior). Furthermore, he was pleasant company. In between I even forgot the pulsating pain in my foot. Ironically enough, while driving through Geneva, he drove right past my newly lost girlfriend's apartment, albeit at two in the morning – a quiet threshold moment that echoed on in the form of a resurfaced ache. Insignificant as it might have appeared, it marked a definitive moment between the last vestiges of my adolescence and the tenor of my future, based on a more conscious quest of values and the paths I would henceforth choose to pursue.

At Emerson College the hitchhiking days dwindled like falling leaves in late autumn. Yet, they were endowed with a sheen like the slow burning colors of fall, starting off with an unforgettable long weekend trip to the Isle of White, followed closely by a memorable trip to Brighton with Tina, my future wife, who I'd met a few weeks into the semester. Whenever she was with me the cars stopped within minutes. I remember very little of the people and cars that picked us up, except for a trip to London when the seventh generation Mr. McMillan from the McMillan publishing empire picked us up in his luxurious Bentley.

Hitchhiking came to an abrupt, decisive, and anti-climactic halt. After Emerson College and before continuing my teacher education studies in Witten-Annen, Germany, I still worked part-time in Basel during the summer to fill up my coffers. In between, I hitchhiked a couple of times up to Bochum to be with Tina, a five to eight-hour trip, depending. On my return journey on my last visit, before moving in with Tina, I stood next to the entrance ramp of the highway for hours, cursing all the passing cars. Then, from one moment to the next I'd had enough; I simply turned my back to the highway, and caught the next train back to Basel. *That's it, I'm done. Never again.* An era had come to an end.

Except, of course, never doesn't necessarily mean never. I did end up hitchhiking a few more times to and from the Waldorf Institute Witten-Annen before we purchased a car, which ended my hitchhiking days once and for all. I do, however, remember my last ride, though it was only a matter of a few minutes and miles. The guy who stopped looked like Ian Anderson from Jethro Tull's heyday. He sucked and puffed feverishly on a self-rolled cigarette, and his long straggly hair kept falling into his slightly bulging eyes and large-pored cheeks, causing him to shake and twitch his head and face to dislodge the offending strands. Recurrently, he looked at me, smiling, which teetered at the cusp of a giggle, lending him a foolish grin. It put me on edge. At length he blurted out, "We're all in disguise!"

"What do you mean?" I wasn't sure how to respond.

"I don't know who you are... you don't know who I am." He tittered, his voice flitting up an octave.

"I suppose so."

"And even if you *did* know me, and if I *did* know you, we still wouldn't know. Not really." He stared, gaging my reaction. I didn't answer. "You seem nice... but you could be a killer. And you don't know if I'm nice." *Did he have something sinister in mind?*

He sucked and puffed loudly, smoke rolling off the dashboard and front window in little mushrooms. I expected him to resume his weird talk, but he slumped into sullen silence.

"You can drop me off at the next corner." I half expected him to continue driving, but he slowed down and stopped. "Thanks a lot."

As I shut the car door he yelled, "We're all in disguise."

I nodded and gave him the thumbs up.

Glossary
South African Words

Agtergat ~ backside, pronounced ACHterCHat, like the German ACHtung, or LoCHness monster
Aikhona ~ (Zulu/Xhosa) emphatic no or disagreement
Amandla ~ (Nguni) Power
Azania ~ Proposed name for South Africa
Biltong ~ Strips of cured and dried meat
blerry ~ Bloody
bliksem ~ a 'bastard' or scoundrel; to hit or beat someone
Boere stad ~ Farmer's town
Boetie ~ Brother; familiar or affectionate form of address
Bokkie ~ Girlfriend; term of endearment
Braaivleis ~ Similar to a barbecue
Bundu ~ Remote area; out in the bush
Cherry ~ Girlfriend; chick
China ~ Friend; buddy, mate
Chommie ~ Friend; chum
Dagga ~ (Khoi) marijuana
Dassies ~ Rock rabbit or hyraxes
Dinkum ~ Really, true, honest (originally Australian)
Donga ~ (Zulu/Xhosa) Dry gulley/ravine formed by erosion
Donner ~ (Thunder) To hit or strike someone
Dorp ~ Village
Gatvol ~ Getting angry; 'I have had enough of you.'
Gogga ~ Bug
Goggatjie ~ Term of endearment, especially children
Hamba Gahle ~ (Zulu/Xhosa) Go well
Indaba ~ Meeting of the community or tribe
Inyanga ~ (Zulu/Xhosa) Healer, herbalist, diviner
Jo'burg, Jozies ~ Johannesburg
Jol ~ Having a good time, to party

Glossary

Jy weet ~ You know
Kiff ~ Very cool, great, wonderful
Knobkerrie ~ A club or stick with a knob at one end
Koppie ~ Small hill
Krantz ~ Steep cliff crowning the top of a mountain
Kwaai ~ Angry (can also mean 'cool')
Laatlammetjie ~ A child born late to parents
mielie-meal ~ Maize meal porridge
Muthi ~ Medicine
Moffie ~ Gay, derogatory expression
Nkosi or Inkosi ~ (Xosa/Zulu) Chief or ruler
Opskud ~ Hurry up
Papgat ~ Weak person
Poepol ~ Idiot (lit. arsehole)
poesie ~ Female genitalia (derogatory)
Regte ~ Real, authentic
Robots ~ Traffic lights
Sala Gahle ~ Stay well
Sangoma ~ (Zulu) Traditional healer, diviner
Spoors ~ Trail, track
Sterre ~ Stars
S'truths ~ In truth
tire-tekkies ~ running shoes/sandals made from old tires
Tokoloshes ~ (Zulu/Xhosa) A little being that invokes fear
Troepie ~ National service person, private soldier
Ubuntu ~ (Xhosa/Zulu) Virtues of essential humanity
Umfundisi ~ Respected person, teacher, priest
Veld ~ Open grassland, semi desert
Vlakte ~ Open and extended flat country
Voetsak ~ Go away, get lost
Waai ~ To go
Zol ~ A joint or a rolled cigarette

Acknowledgements

I would like to express my heartfelt appreciation to all the people who contributed to the creation of *Fringe Locations* in one way or another: Leif Garbisch for reading the first draft of the book and his astute editorial comments, Patrick Stolfo for incisive remarks and copyediting, and especially my wife, Martina Angela Müller, whose insightful statements and sharp observations helped shape many of these stories. Furthermore, I am greatly indebted to the editors of the magazines and journals in which some of these stories first appeared, and for their constructive and valuable feedback. Lastly, I would like to recognize all the people who appear in this book or who inspired some of the stories. They are housed in a special location within me.

Publication Credits

The following stories first appeared in the following publications:

"Pool Cleaner from the Yucatan," *The Literary Yard;* "Up in Smoke," *The Autumn Sound Review;* "Sundial," *Spinozablue;* "Yeah, I Killed My Girlfriend," *The Flash Offensive;* "Optimistic Freshman," *Journal of Microliterature;* "Hotel Pischa," *Postcard Shorts;* "4'33"," *ink sweat and tears;* "Stromboli," *About Place Journal;* "The Red Wind," *Halfway Down the Stairs;* A Walk through Snow and Time," *Outside In Literary Travel Magazine;* "Water, Water," *The Blue Hour Magazine;* "Thumbing Down the Road," *Eonia Review;* "Draft Dodger" and "Allen Ginsberg at the Atlantis" were first published in *Rites of Rock* (Adonis Press) in a slightly altered form.

About the Author

Eric G. Müller was born in Durban, South Africa. After graduating from the University of the Witwatersrand, Johannesburg, South Africa, he continued his studies in England and Germany, focusing on drama, music, and education. He is the director of Teacher Education at the Alkion Center, and a humanities teacher at the Hawthorne Valley High School in Harlemville, New York. He has published numerous books, including novels, children's books, and poetry.

www.ericgmuller.com
www.alkion-press.com

www.ingramcontent.com/pod-product-compliance
Lightning Source LLC
Chambersburg PA
CBHW021112080526
44587CB00010B/490